W9-CAF-998

ERGONOMICS MADE EASY

✔ *A Checklist* ✔
Approach

Deborah Kearney

Government Institutes
Rockville, Maryland

Government Institutes, Inc., 4 Research Place, Rockville, Maryland 20850, USA.

Copyright © 1998 by Government Institutes. All rights reserved.

02 01 00 99   5 4 3 2

No part of this work may be reproduced or transmitted in any form or by any means, electronic or mechanical, including photocopying, recording, or any information storage and retrieval system, without permission in writing from the publisher. All requests for permission to reproduce material from this work should be directed to Government Institutes, Inc., 4 Research Place, Rockville, Maryland 20850, USA.

The reader should not rely on this publication to address specific questions that apply to a particular set of facts. The author and publisher make no representation or warranty, express or implied, as to the completeness, correctness or utility of the information in this publication. In addition, the author and publisher assume no liability of any kind whatsoever resulting from the use of or reliance upon the contents of this book.

Library of Congress Cataloging-in-Publication Data

Kearney, Deborah S.
Ergonomics made easy : a checklist approach / by Deborah Kearney.
            p.   cm.
      Includes bibliographical references and index.
      ISBN: 0-86587-591-X
      1. Human engineering.   I. Title.
  TA166.K39   1998
   620.8'2--dc21
                                97-47121
                                CIP

Printed in the United States of America

Table of Contents

List of Figures and Tables

Ergonomic Design for Safety Managers

The Goal of This Guide

The goal of this guide is to increase the knowledge of safety managers in the use of ergonomics.

Four objectives are pursued:

1. Provide recommendations about the critical ergonomic design factors.

2. Identify the necessity of including ergonomics in all phases of project management.

3. Identify the necessity of using ergonomics to maintain a competitive edge in order to increase client base and client satisfaction.

4. Provide ergonomic design information to allow engineers, architects and designers to develop accurate cost comparisons.

In order to fulfill these objectives, this guide provides an illustrated review of the human body and its relation to design factors, with statistical information. It is designed to allow the safety manager to evaluate each design factor within the project's parameters in order to determine;

> 1. cost-effectiveness,

2. implementation strategy
3. human factors
4. maintenance and operation outcomes, and
5. visual image and integration issues.

This guide is intended to educate and inform before and beyond the technical requirements of job safety analysis.

About the Author

Deborah Kearney, Ph.D., is president of Work Stations Inc., a design and manufacturing firm specializing in creating environments, furnishings, and adaptive and assistive devices for industries, schools, health care facilities, and individuals. She is also Executive Director of the SafeWork Institute, a member of the Human Factors and Ergonomics Society, the American Society of Safety Engineers, the American Psychological Association, and the International Facilities Management Association. Dr. Kearney is an internationally-recognized expert on ergonomics, human factors engineering, workstation design, and disability accomodation. She is the award-winning author of *Reasonable Accomodations: Job Descriptions in the Age of ADA, OSHA, and Workers' Comp*, *The ADA in Practice*, and *The New ADA: Compliance and Costs*. Dr. Kearney received her masters and doctoral degrees in psychology from the University of Massachusetts-Amherst.

Ergonomics and Safety Management

The goal of safety managers is to manage facilities so that people can safely accomplish the objectives of their employment. The planning and achievement of productive environments for people is an art and a science. Melding the art and the science of production with that of safety management is a recent development driven by the demands of ever-increasing statutes, codes, regulations, standards and laws. The current legal trend is toward increased sensitivity to the rights of individuals in the workplace (e.g. the Americans with Disabilities Act of 1990 and OSHA's ergonomic initiatives.) Citations for ergonomic violations currently fall under Section 5 of the 1972 OSHA Law.

OSHA and Ergonomics

Ergonomic violations fall under the General Duty Clause of the Occupational Safety and Health Act of 1970.

Section 5

A. Each Employer
Shall furnish to each employee a place of employment that is free from any recognized hazards that may cause or is likely to cause death or serious harm.
B. Each Employee
Shall comply with Occupational Safety and Health (OSH) Standards and all rules, regulations, and orders pursuant to the act that are applicable to his/her own actions and conduct.

Introduction

Safety managers are increasingly being asked to include ergonomics in their programs. To do this, they must have the ability to work within both a legal and a human-factors framework. The proposals of architectural designers and vendors are now being evaluated by safety management against a broad criteria of considerations, of which technology and human factors are the key. The evaluation includes the following factors:

- Company philosophy
- Creativity
- Customer satisfaction
- History of performance
- Incorporation of the Total Design Process
- Local government relationships
- Maintenance management systems
- National and international capabilities
- Performance-based contracts
- Product life cycle and costs
- Reliability of "should" cost estimates
- Schedule demands
- Size and financial strength
- Staffing/organization
- Technical ability
- Total Quality Management Program
- Training
- Understanding of legal compliance issues and constraints
- Variety of design services
- Working relationships with contractors and vendors (85% of a project's cost is materials and field labor)

Today, safety managers must offer their organizations a variety of specialized services. In addition to traditional needs, safety now requires a wide range of management services that match its strategic plans in a cost-effective manner. Satisfying these organizational needs means ensuring that every factor of services, whether centered on form or function, meets the necessities of the end-user in terms of ergonomics. Successful ergonomic design results from an understanding and concern for the needs of these end-users. Ergonomic success is therefore reflected in the employees' ability to productively and efficiently use machines, equipment, tools, and instruments in workplace environments without stress or fatigue.

The importance of ergonomics in safety management is that it allows the criteria of human factors to be a priority for each working environment. That is an important consideration in today's society, since one in five workers will experience temporary or permanent functional limitations at some time during their work life.

Statistics of Note:

- 57.7 million Americans have difficulty performing the daily activities of sitting, standing, reaching, and fingering.
- The mean age of American workers in the year 2000 will be 45.

Managers must use the elements of human-factors engineering to design user-friendly environments that are safe and fulfill OSHA requirements. Safety management that incorporates ergonomics will ultimately result in practical, cost-effective, and enduring implementations that meet production and safety objectives. The ideal design goes beyond the transient qualities of style and accommodates the vicissitudes of life.

Ergonomics and Design

Ergonomic design in safety management is the application of human factors engineering to the elements of form (structure) and function (ambience). The physical environment must accommodate the widest range of human functional limitations to enhance the usability of any area. Cost-effectiveness in ergonomics is a result of design incentives. Good design costs no more than bad design. For example, operating controls at heights that do not require over-reaching makes good ergonomic and economic sense because it reduces the amount of wiring necessary and also lessens installation time. Likewise, energy-efficient task lighting reduces energy consumption and increases the visual acuity of people with limited vision. A well-planned acoustical system in conjunction with the ventilation system can increase the creativity and comfort in areas designed for groups of varying numbers. Creating safe environments can include using ergonomics as a guide to choices of flooring and finishes by helping to reduce the number-one injury in America—slips and falls.

Ergonomics and Design

For exterior entrances, if a main entrance is set 6" above grade, a sloped walkway will meet the needs of most people and reduce the cost of elaborate ramps used to bypass steps. For interior entranes to lobbies and passageways, consider the use of color, textures, slip-resistant floor finishes, removal of obstructions, and aids for balance. In addition to the gains made for the safety of users, ergonomics can make a facility easier to maintain. By qualifying materials for durability and longevity, injury, repairs, and maintenance are reduced. The overalll form and function of a workplace environment can be improved with ergonomically sound design.

Ergonomic designs should be subtle and perceived as an enhancement to the end-users' capabilities. Control over one's environmental comfort and safety is the desired outcome of ergonomics. When ergonomic designs were first introduced, the engineering emphasis was on manufacturing productivity. Now ergonomic designs are available that support safety management goals with effective and attractive solutions meeting compliance guidelines.

The successful safety manager is a team player who will partner with designers and vendors to introduce ergonomic designs to organizations that allow them to be more competitive. A successful safety manager is one that uses technical excellence to balance costs, technologies, and the needs of people to provide an adaptable and flexible environment.

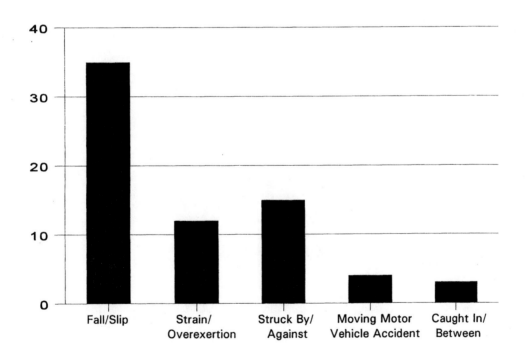

Figure 1. Total Number of Injured Workers Categorized by Type of Injury.

Designing for Aging, Disability, Disease, and Injury

Most people who have functional limitations still lead active lives. They work and live independently, and engage in social leisure activities. To provide these people with environments that support their work activities, safety managers need to understand their needs. This means going beyond traditional design standards that have been based on normative data of weight, height, age, and range of motion. The design difficulty here is that relying on norms does not take into consideration how the body with functional limitations performs required tasks. That is why it is important to balance design and ergonomics as integral parts of safety management.

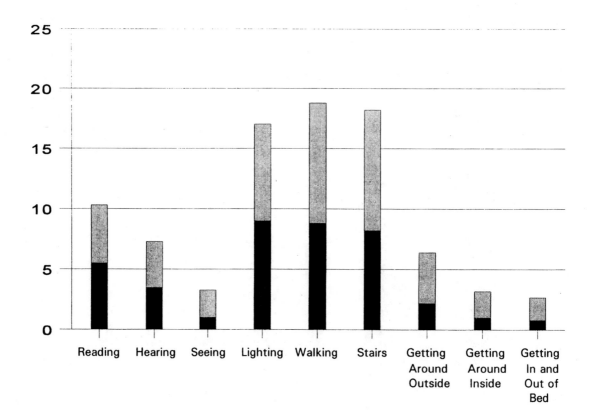

Figure 2. Routine Activities that a Percentage of the Population Find Difficult.

Designing for a Talented Aging Workforce

The goal here is to design for a decline in strength, stamina, visual acuity, for gait impairments, and the limitations of hearing that frequently occur with an aging workforce. The following graphs and figures are illustrative of this need.

Aging

During this century, the average life expectancy rate has increased at a dramatic rate. In 1900 in the United States, the average life expectancy rate was 47 years. By 1980 it was 75 years, and has increased slightly since then. This increase in life expectancy means that there there are many more aging workers available for the work force than were present 100 years ago.

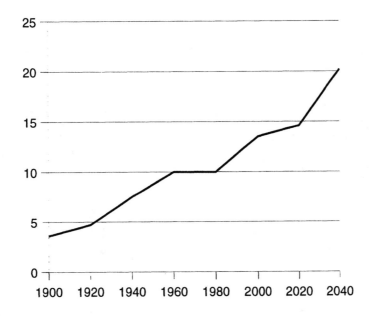

Figure 3. Projected Percentage Growth of the U.S. Population over the Age of 65.

Designing and Aging

Physical Changes:

The physical changes that are experienced during the aging process generally involve mobility, strength and stamina, vision, hearing, and tactile and thermal sensitivity. The degree of change experienced in each of those areas can vary widely. Ergonomic design can increase the sense of orientation by providing appropriate forms of physical support and behavioral cues. Sensory impairment, for example, does not necessarily mean that the worker cannot respond to environmental information. But aging workers may require more reaction time and may need clearer and stronger stimuli to compensate for the loss of sensitivity. The degree to which immediate surroundings promote or hinder appropriate action depends in large part on the severity of sensory losses and the combinations of impairments.

Mobility:

A number of factors—many of them products of a lifetime of physical wear and tear—force many older workers to perform tasks more slowly. Gravity, for example, can gradually overcome our ability to stand perfectly erect, and the stooped posture of aging can itself cause difficulty in walking, sitting down, standing up, and turning. Reductions in ambulatory speed may be caused by a slowed reaction time; low energy levels resulting from such chronic conditions as heart disease; inner-ear damage resulting in a loss of balance or poor feedback about the position of body and limbs; and losses of vision and hearing.

Strength and Stamina:

Strength may decrease with age, but often endurance—or stamina—remains relatively strong. When mobility is hindered, though, reduced strength and stamina are commonplace. Joints normally become more rigid with advancing age. Muscle strength and coordination almost always decrease. Overhead cabinets and shelves are suddenly beyond reach. Round knobs may become hard to grasp and manipulate. And because once simple movements may now require more exertion of strength and stamina, distances in both interior and exterior layouts can become important considerations.

Visual Acuity:

Vision begins to decline as early as age 40, and long-term impairment can include loss of visual field and acuity, reduced color sensitivity, and increased sensitivity to glare. Older workers may require up to twice as much light as younger workers to achieve equal visual acuity. Colors of similar intensity are more difficult to differentiate from one another, especially when viewed against similarly textured or reflective surfaces and when viewed under uniform lighting conditions. Pastels, very dark shades, and combinations of blues and greens can be particularly difficult for older workers. These problems can be addressed in ergonomic design through increased illumination levels, increased size for signs, heightened contrast between elements in all visually presented information, and the use of highly contrasting colors. Other visual changes occurring in older workers include declines in the ability to see fine detail, to distinguish depth, and to adapt to changes in brightness. Glare is often a major problem; the distraction it causes can affect balance, orientation, attention span, and short-term memory. Glare is often caused by unshielded artificial lighting or by direct sunlight, which beams onto a reflective interior space.

Hearing:

Hearing ability often begins to decline noticeably even earlier than visual acuity does. Older workers frequently find it difficult to hear higher frequency sounds, such as those emitted by bells, and fire and smoke sirens. Designers should always consider redundant-cueing safety systems—systems that issue alarms in both audible (in the lower frequencies) and visible modes, for example.

A decline in hearing also typically makes it difficult for a person to discern one voice or one sound against a background of competing sounds or voices; thus, sound control becomes an important general design issue.

Tactile and Thermal Sensitivity:

Sensitivity to touch naturally and normally declines with age because the skin becomes drier and less elastic. Thus, subtle changes in environmental texture can go unnoticed by older employees. The ability to smell—though not a tactile issue—often declines with touch; sensitivity remains high enough, however, to make odor control important.

Also important among the common tactile losses of aging are declines in immediate sensitivity to pain and temperature.

Designing and Disability

Americans over the age of 15 with one or more functional impairments represent more than one in every five people, or 37.3 million of 180 million total population. In addition,

The probability of individuals over 65 having difficulty performing a basic activity is four times greater than in individuals between the ages of 15 and 64. The task for safety managers is to check each work area design and product specification to determine the usability, enhancement, and conditions of the safety provided. For example, a bordered rug can appear to an employee with low vision as if it were a step down. This optical illusion can create an unsafe condition and cause a fall.

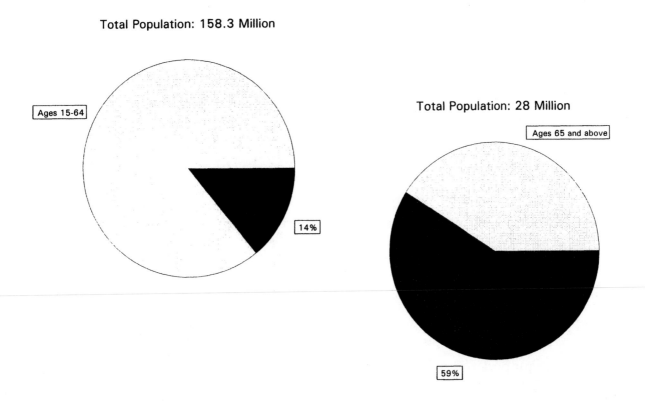

Figure 4. Percentage of Americans with Functional Limitations.

How the Body Works

Ergonomics, Work, Energy:

Energy is the ability to do work. When work is done, energy is used or converted from one form to another.

To an ergonomist, work is done only when a force moves something. If you lift a heavy object, you do work because you exert a force that moves that object. Work cannot be done without energy. How the body "works" is critical to ergonomics. Understanding the work of the body requires understanding energy and movement.

Energy Requirements:

Energy is measured in units called joules. The joule is a small unit: there are 1,000 joules in a kilojoule (kj)—a unit used for measuring the amount of energy in our food. Kilocalories (kcal) are also used to measure energy. One kilocalorie is equal to 4.2 kilojoules. Men and women, children, teenagers, and adults all use different amounts of energy every day, and it depends on what their activities are and how much they weigh. An average teenage boy needs about 3,000 kcal (12,600 kj) of energy each day, while a teenage girl needs about 2,500 kcal (10,500 kj).

Food Energy:

Safety management includes evaluating food and beverage sources for work areas that support the energy needs of workers. While would not be able to stay alive without the energy you get from food, it can be just as harmful for you to consume too much energy as too little. Different kinds of food contain different amounts of energy. For example, you would have to eat about 2.2 lb (1 kg) of fresh tomatoes to get as much energy as you would from just 0.8 oz (24 g) milk chocolate.

Potential Energy:

The energy we gain from food is converted to use as we work. Potential energy is the energy that a body contains in storage because of its position or state. For example, a jack-in-the-box has tremendous potential energy when it is squashed into its box. Types of potential energy are gravitational potential energy (of a raised object), elastic potential energy (of a stretched or squashed elastic material), electrical potential energy (of an object near an electric charge), and magnetic potential energy (of a magnetic object near a magnet).

Power Lifting:

Power is the rate at which work is done or how quickly one form of energy is changed to another. Generally, a man is more powerful than a child is. He can lift a larger load and lift more quickly than the average child. The unit of power is the watt, which equals 1 joule per second.

Inclined Plane:

It is easier to push something up a slope, or inclined plane, than to lift it straight up. Movers use a ramp to load heavy items into a truck. They have to move things further than they would if they lifted them vertically, but the movement uses less energy. An inclined plane is therefore a force magnifier.

Energy and Movement

Lever:

A lever is a rod or bar that turns around a point called the fulcrum, or pivot, to move a load. There are three kinds of levers, with different arrangements of load, effort, and fulcrum. Some levers magnify force, others magnify distance. For a lever to be a force magnifier, the effort must be applied farther away from the fulcrum than the load. There are examples of levers in your body. For example, your arm is a Class 3 lever. Your elbow is the fulcrum, the muscles in your arm provide the effort, and your hand is the load.

Magnifying Force:

Archimedes, the ancient Greek inventor, said, "Give me a lever long enough, and I could move the world." In theory, this statement is true because a lever magnifies force. For example, a claw hammer, a type of lever, can be used to remove a nail from a piece of wood because of the magnified force the lever provides.

Magnifying Movement:

When rowers use their oars to move a boat, they are using machines that magnify movement. They move the inner end of the oars a small distance, but the outer end of the oars moves a greater distance, pulling the boat swiftly through the water.

These simple overviews on energy are critical to understanding how the body is formed to function while working.

The Brain: Structural Plan and Functions of the Cerebrum:

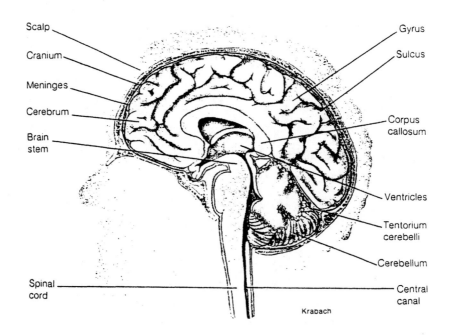

Figure 5. The Brain.

The brain is composed of an enormous number of association neurons, with accompanying neuroglia, arranged into brain regions and divisions. These neurons receive sensory information, direct the activity of motor neurons, and perform such higher brain functions as learning and memory. Even self-awareness, emotions, and consciousness may derive from complex interactions of different brain regions.

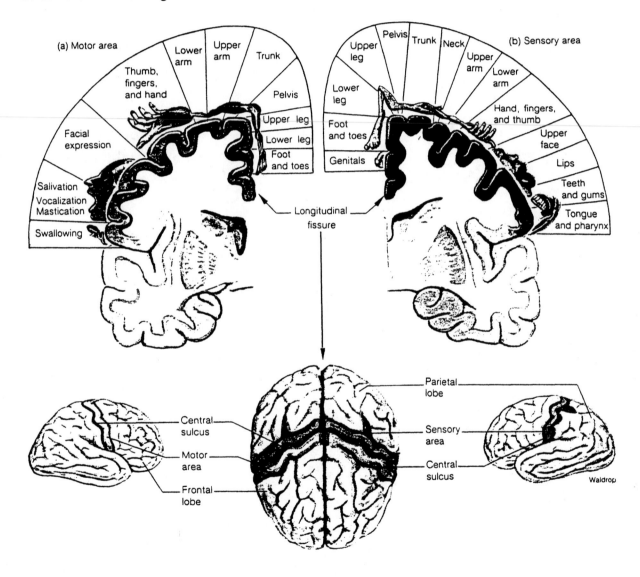

Figure 6. Motor and Sensory Areas of the Brain.

The Central Nervous System (CNS) consists of the brain and the spinal cord, both of which are covered with meninges and bathed in cerebrospinal fluid.

Motor and sensory areas of the cerebral cortex are a) motor areas that control skeletal muscles, and b) sensory areas that receive somatesthetic sensations.

Front Skeleton:

Under the skin and muscles is the skeleton—a tough, flexible bone structure, which supports and protects the body.

The front part of the skeleton is made up of the face bones of the skull, the collar bones, the breast bone, and the ribs. The hard skull protects the brain, like a shell around a walnut, and the ribs shield the heart and lungs.

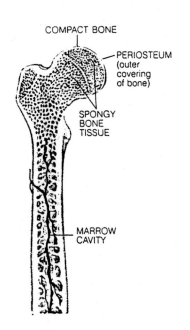

Figure 7. Interior Structure of Bones.

Although bones appear hard and dry, they are made up of living cells, blood vessels, and nerves. Most bones have three layers. A thin, tough outer shell, called the periosteum, covers a strong layer of hard bone that surrounds a lighter, spongy core. The periosteum is made of cells that can replace and repair broken bone. This hard layer contains calcium salts that make the bone strong. The inner layer of spongy bone is like a honeycomb, so that the bone is lightweight.

Some larger bones, such as the breast bone and the thigh bones, contain a soft, jelly-like substance, called marrow, in the spongy core. Bone marrow can produce as many as 5 billion red blood cells in just one day.

Back Skeleton:

The back skeleton gives the body strength. The spine, the pelvis, the arms and legs, together with the front skeleton, protect all the body's important parts. The bones of the back skeleton, with muscles attached to them, enable the body to move.

Bones cannot bend, but when two bones meet they form a moveable joint. A smooth tissue called cartilage covers the ends of the bones. This protects the bones from wearing away. Around most joints is a sac that contains synovial fluid, which keeps bones from grinding together. Strong elastic fibers, called ligaments, hold the two bones of the joint together. The joint moves when muscles pull on either of the bones.

There are several types of joints that permit different kinds and degrees of motion. Hinge joints, most notably in elbows and knees, swing back and forth like doors on hinges. Ball-and-socket joints—the shoulder and hip—allow one bone to twist and turn in many directions while remaining firmly connected to another.

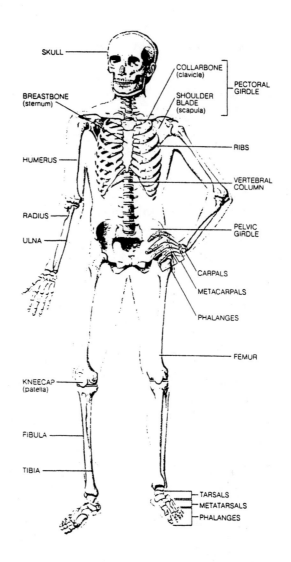

Figure 8. Basic Human Skeleton.

Inside the Spine:

The spine consists of 24 bones, called the vertebrae, sacrum, and coccyx. It keeps the body upright, but it is not a stiff rod. Soft, tough discs of cartilage act as cushions between the vertebrae so that the spine can twist and bend. The spine protects the spinal cord.

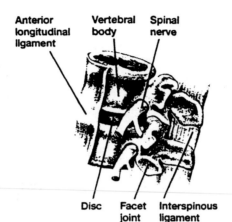

Figure 9. The Human Spine.

Musculoskeletal Ailments

Bones, muscles, ligaments, tendons, and joints are natural marvels of engineering and construction, which have evolved over millions of years to provide strength, control, and flexibility. Evolution, however, has not caught up with human invention; our bodies are simply not designed to handle many of the physical stresses of modern life. Activities such as plucking chickens, typing at a word processor, or gliding cans and bottles through the supermarket checkout counter for eight hours each day can tax the human body's musculoskeletal system beyond its capacity to absorb stress, resulting in physical damage.

These days, ailments of bones and muscles due to environmental stresses are extensive. Back pain affects 5.4 million Americans each year, costs $16 billion annually for treatment, and is cited in 30 to 40 percent of all workers' compensation claims, according to the Office of Ergonomics at the Occupational Safety and Health Administration (OSHA). Overuse disorders—wear and tear on joints and tendons that comes from repeating the same motion hour after hour, day after day—affect six out of ever one-hundred workers. In some industries, such as meatpacking and automobile assembly, more than one-third of the employees complain of these ailments.

The Basic Anatomy of the Musculoskeletal System:

We may think of bones and muscles as different from inorganic materials such as steel or glass, but in many ways they are very similar. Just as excess stress causes glass to shatter, a sudden force can break a bone. Just as the cumulative effects of rust and vibration will cause a steel girder in a bridge to fall, so can a lifetime of small injuries can add up to produce osteoarthritis in a joint. We do have a built-in advantage over bridges and buildings because our bones and muscles can adapt to stress. They can remodel their structures, heal when at rest, and be trained to respond more effectively to environmental demands. The bones, joints, muscles, tendons, ligaments, cartilage, and bursas of the human body have evolved sophisticated strategies to respond to varying stresses while supporting us and providing protection for other body organs.

Musculoskeletal disorders can be seen as responses to overloads on the body, caused in varying degrees by unhealthy levels of physical stress in the environment. Looked at in this way, prevention of these injuries boils down to reducing the amount of stress to which the system is exposed and/or increasing the amount of stress each system can tolerate through such interventions as exercise, better diet, and improved habits. This is why safety management includes training in such areas as stretch breaks at work, break rooms with healthy food and beverage choices, and job safety analysis techniques.

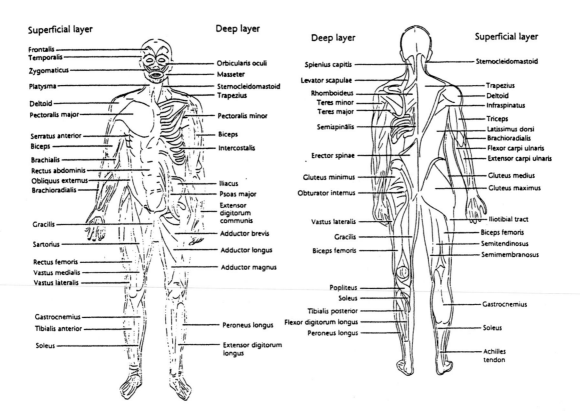

Figure 10. The Muscle System.

Bones:

The skeleton is living scaffolding that gives the body structure and strength. The 206 bones of the human skeleton not only give the human body its shape and form, but protect delicate organs, such as the heart and the brain; act as reservoirs for essential elements, such as calcium and phosphorous; provide a site for the production of important blood cells; and provide the levers, articulation, and locations for the attachments of muscles that allow movement.

The bones of the skeletal system are divided into four classifications: long, short, flat, and irregular. The shape of each type of bone suits it to respond to different environmental stresses. For example, the round shape of the skull gives it extra strength to protect the brain, while the bones of the spine thicken as they progress down the back, enabling them to support extra weight.

The Spine:

The spine consists of thirty-three bones, called vertebrae, which are classified into five separate regions: the cervical spine (neck area)—seven vertebrae that support the head and protect the spinal cord on its way up to the head; the thoracic spine—twelve vertebrae, each connected to rib bones; the lumbar spine—five lumbar vertebrae, which are slightly larger than the other vertebrae because they are designed to bear much of the weight of the body (the lower back is the most common site of back pain); the sacrum or sacral vertebrae— five fused bones at the base of the spine; and the coccygeal vertebrae—four vertebrae that comprise the coccyx, or tailbone.

In their stacked alignment, the vertebrae surround a central canal containing the spinal cord, the major nerve trunk for the body and the seat of reflexes. Also passing through the vertebrae are the nerves leading from the spinal cord to the limbs and other organs. The openings between vertebrae that these nerves pass through can become injured—a common cause of pinched nerves.

Joints:

The joints, which connect two moving bones together to allow motion and provide stability, have evolved into three types, each with its own biomechanical advantage.

The three types of joints are: fibrous joints, such as those in the skull, which have very limited motion and provide stability; cartilaginous joints, such as those between vertebrae, which allow some motion in the spine; and synovial joints, such as those found in the elbow, wrist, and knee, which are the most common type and allow the greatest degree of movement.

Which Joint Is Most Vulnerable:

The knee is the body's biggest and heaviest joint and seems well armored because it is wrapped in a protective, fluid-filled bag called the synovial capsule. Its parts are lashed together with tendons and ligaments. It is protected by a stout bony shield—the kneecap. The thighbone is cushioned from contact with the lower-leg bones by shock-absorbing cartilage. Despite all of this protection, the knee is injured more often than any other joint.

When the knee is either knocked or wrenched out of position, and ligaments either tear or are stretched too far, the kneecap is sometimes dislocated, and the cartilage inside the joint may be damaged. The most dramatic example of knee injury is the blind-side tackle in football, in which a runner's knee is forcibly rammed sideways.

Muscles

The more than 600 muscles in the human body make movement possible and perform such crucial functions as pumping blood and inhaling and exhaling air. They also generate heat, enable us to sit and stand, and protect bones by absorbing impacts to the body.

The best-known and most common types of muscles—the skeletal muscles—make up about 40 percent of body weight. These muscles are also called voluntary muscles because they are under conscious control. The other two types of muscles—visceral and cardiac—are involuntary muscles that work without conscious control. Visceral muscles are involved in the function of internal organs, such as the stomach, intestines, uterus, and blood vessels. They are not attached to bone, act slowly, and can remain contracted for long periods of time. Cardiac muscles are found only in the heart and make up much of the heart wall.

Ligaments:

Ligaments are long bands of collagen fibers arranged in parallel bundles that hold bones to other bones and give a joint stability, allowing movement in some directions while restricting it in others. Ligaments can be found encircling the hip joint and parallel to the ends of bones in the knee joint, where they provide strength and stability.

How Do Hip, Thigh, and Knee Relate to One Another?

The bones of the hip, thigh, and knee are much stronger and heavier than those of the arms, and the muscles that control them are thus much larger. At the hips, two large, flaring bones form the pelvis, a basin-shaped structure that cradles and protects vital organs. At the lower end of the pelvis are two large socket joints into which fit the bulbous upper ends of your thighbones—the longest, strongest bones in the body. The thighbones, in turn, fit into the knee joints, which connect the body's midsection to the shinbones and feet.

Tendons:

Tendons are cordlike bundles of fibers found at the ends of muscles that attach muscles to bones. Tendons enable muscles to move the attached bone, sometimes at a distance. Tendon cells are arranged in parallel bundles, which gives them high tensile strength while allowing them to transmit force from muscle to bone without getting damaged. The length of tendons ranges from less than 1 inch to more than 1 foot, the longest being the Achilles tendon, which runs from the heel to the calf.

How Does the Foot Work?

The foot is a flexible collection of soft, breakable bones. Yet it can easily handle the jarring weight of a whole body because all of these bones are held firmly in place by a web of sinewy muscles and strong ligaments that have great tensile strength. This combination of bones and bindings makes for an extraordinarily springy, flexible structure. The wide, flat, bandagelike ligaments that encircle the ankle joints act like the ankle supports an ice skater might wear. As the impact of body weight spreads out through the tarsal bones, the foot's arch softens the shock, turning it into a "bounce" that makes walking much easier.

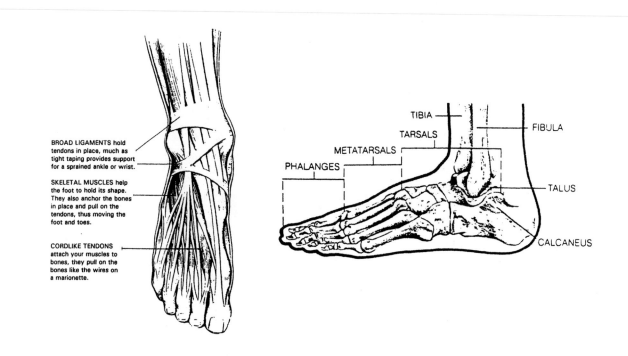

BROAD LIGAMENTS hold tendons in place, much as tight taping provides support for a sprained ankle or wrist.

SKELETAL MUSCLES help the foot to hold its shape. They also anchor the bones in place and pull on the tendons, thus moving the foot and toes.

CORDLIKE TENDONS attach your muscles to bones, they pull on the bones like the wires on a marionette.

TIBIA

FIBULA

TARSALS

METATARSALS

PHALANGES

TALUS

CALCANEUS

Figure 11. Structure of the Foot.

When a runner lands on his or her foot, the weight descends from the tibia, a leg bone, into the talus (meaning "ankle bone"). The weight is distributed forward to the tarsals and metatarsals and backward to the heel bone (calcaneus). All of the joints' surfaces are subject to wear, tear, and arthritis. The arches form a "springy" shock-absorbing system.

Cartilage:

Cartilage is a type of connective tissue made up of specialized cells called chondrocytes, which are embedded in a matrix of varying amounts of collagen. There are three types of cartilage: hyaline cartilage—a tough, smooth tissue that provides a low-friction coating for the bony ends of joints; fibrocartilage—a solid, strong collagen found in the intervertebral disks between the bones of the spine; and elastic cartilage—a soft and rubbery substance found in such places as the outer ear and the epiglottis.

Injuries and Ergonomics

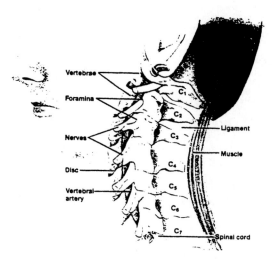

Figure 12. Structure of the Neck.

The Neck:

The neck (cervical spine) is made up of the top seven vertebrae of the spine. A healthy neck is strong, flexible, and pain free, and the joints of these vertebrae are balanced and aligned with a natural curve. The neck supports the head, protects the spinal cord and spinal nerves, and allows movement of the head in a variety of ways.

Vertebrae and Discs:

The neck is made up of seven bones (vertebrae), naturally alighted in a slight forward curve. The vertebrae have openings where the cervical nerves pass into the shoulders and arms. Discs are shock-absorbing pads of cartilage between the vertebrae. Healthy discs have a tough covering, a jelly-like interior, and a certain amount of "give" to adapt to various head and neck movements.

Joints:

The joints in the neck allow movement of the head. Each vertebra joins with the next in two places, giving the spine great flexibility.

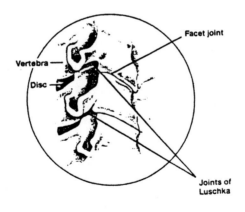

Figure 13. Structure of Joints.

Nerves:

The neck is the channel connecting the brain with the nerves throughout the body. Spinal nerves branch off from the foramina. Each spinal nerve is "rooted" to the spinal cord with two small nerve roots.

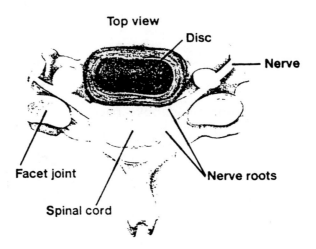

Figure 14. Nerve Structure.

Soft Tissue:

Soft tissue includes muscles, tendons, and ligaments. Muscles work together to move and support the head. Tendons are tough tissues connecting muscle to bone. Ligaments are strong bands of tissue that stabilize and connect the vertebrae.

Trigger Points:

Trigger points are small, localized areas of pain and muscle spasm, a common symptom of many neck problems. Referred pain may originate in the neck but can be felt nearby in the shoulders, arms, hands, or face. Each muscle has its own pattern of referred pain.

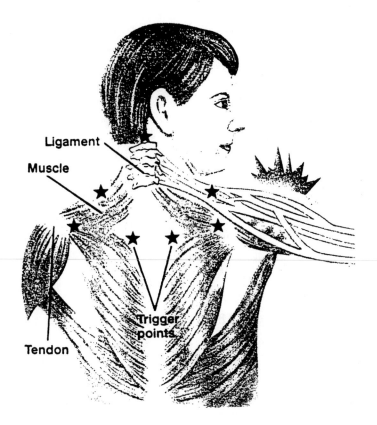

Figure 15. Locations of Trigger Points.

Range of Motion:

The neck moves more than any other part of the spine, and can move in three basic ways. Each of these movements has its own range of motion—the amount of motion that is normally possible. Most neck problems affect the range of motion in some way.

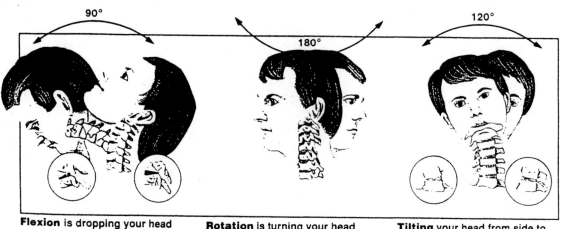

Flexion is dropping your head forward; **extension** is dropping your head backward. Their combined range of motion is about 90°.

Rotation is turning your head from side to side, and has a range of motion of about 180°.

Tilting your head from side to side has a range of motion of about 120°.

Figure 16. Movements of the Neck.

Degenerative Joint Disease:

When a spinal joint becomes misaligned or injured, the vertebrae can't move properly, discs can become compressed, and nerves may be irritated. As degeneration progresses, the discs lose their ability to cushion and the vertebrae can develop bone spurs. Workers may experience pain, stiffness, headaches and nagging neck aches (often worse in the morning). Joint degeneration is often the result of too much stress on the joints caused by poor posture, repeated movements, or injury. Left untreated, joint problems can begin to affect the nerves and spinal cord.

Shoulder Parts:

Like all joints, the shoulder is comprised of many parts. The shoulder joint includes bone, cartilage, a bursa lining, nerves, and many muscles, tendons, and ligaments that hold it together. The shoulder is particularly fragile because its exceptional flexibility and mobility make it vulnerable to wear and tear.

The Shoulder in Motion:

Whether workers are computer operators or plumbers, weekend athletes or cheerleaders, it is the shoulder that allows the arms and hands to function with a wide range of motion. Figure 17 shows the ways strong, flexible muscles keep the shoulder moving safely.

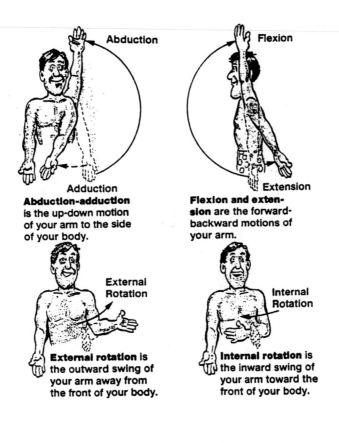

Abduction-adduction is the up-down motion of your arm to the side of your body.

Flexion and extension are the forward-backward motions of your arm.

External rotation is the outward swing of your arm away from the front of your body.

Internal rotation is the inward swing of your arm toward the front of your body.

Figure 17. Movements of the Shoulder.

The Shoulder in Trouble:

Overuse or underuse of the shoulder can cause pain and stiffness, leading to immobility. This, in turn, causes muscle weakness and adhesions around the joint, which further limit mobility and cause more pain. And so the cycle goes until one day the shoulder stops working. Treatment, safe use, and exercise can break the "shoulder in trouble" cycle.

What Causes Knee Problems?

The knee is a complex joint where the upper leg bone (femur) and the lower leg bone (tibia) meet. The kneecap protects the joint. Repeated strain on the joint, an injury, poor posture, or a misaligned joint in the foot ankle, or spine can damage the tissue in the knee. This leads to swelling, stiffness, pain, and sometimes locking or "giving way."

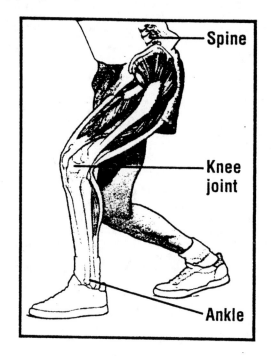

Figure 18. Movement of Knees.

A Healthy Knee:

Ligaments connect the bones and help brace the joint by limiting forward and sideways motions and rotation. Muscles, connected to the bones by tendons, provide strength for movement.

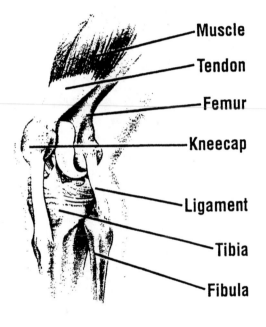

Figure 19. Structure of the Knee.

An Injured Knee:

Long-term wear, overuse, or a sudden injury, such as twisting the knee, can cause the muscles or tendons to over-stretch or the ligaments to tear. The bones may twist, causing a misaligned joint.

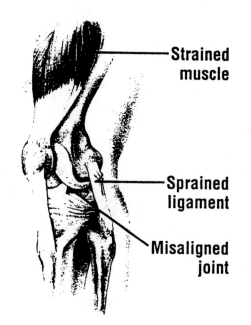

Figure 20. An Injured Knee.

A Closer Look at Joints:

Pivot joints, such as the wrist, can twist and turn. Hinge joints, such as the knee and elbow, move backward and forward. Ball-and-socket joints, such as the hip and shoulder, allow the greatest all-round movement.

Unhealthy Spines:

An unhealthy spine often starts with an unhealthy habit like poor posture. Standing, sitting, or moving incorrectly puts extra stress on the spine and discs, causing pain. Over time, poor posture can even cause the discs to wear out early. Like wrung-out, brittle sponges, the discs lose their ability to cushion the spine, allowing a wide variety of painful spine and disc problems to develop. Unless corrected, they make the spine more vulnerable to reinjury. Fortunately, ergonomics can prevent and even correct many of these problems by changing worker habits with changes in methods, machine, materials, equipment, tools, and instruments.

Poor Posture Backfires:

Sooner or later, poor posture backfires, causing pain by putting the three natural curves out of alignment. Too much slouching puts pressure on the annulus. A swayback posture can overload and inflame the facets. Muscles tighten and may go into spasm to "splint" the spine, adding to the pain workers feel.

How Discs Wear Out:

Over time, the discs may wear out from natural aging. But poor posture can make them wear out early. As discs narrow and dry out, vertebrae come closer together and become irritated. Bony outgrowths may form, narrowing the foramen and irritating nearby nerves.

What Causes Sciatica?

Sciatic is an inflammation of the sciatic nerve, the longest nerve in the body. It runs from your lower spine, through the buttocks, and into the leg and foot. When the sciatic nerve is inflamed, it can cause numbness, tingling, pain, or weakness in the lower back and leg.

Inflamed Joint:

If a bone in the lower back isn't moving properly or is out of position, the joint can become inflamed and irritate the sciatic nerve.

Bulging Disc:

If one of the cushions between the vertebrae is bulging, it can irritate or put pressure on the sciatic nerve.

Muscle Spasm:

If a muscle in the lower back or buttocks is inflamed or tightening, it can irritate or put pressure on the sciatic nerve.

What Causes Foot and Ankle Problems?

The foot is built to withstand motion and pressure. Bones provide the framework. Soft tissue—muscles, tendons, and ligaments—keep the bones stable and control movement. Bones and nerves in the leg connect the foot to the spine. Too many hours on the feet, sudden movements, or misaligned joints can lead to soft tissue and other problems.

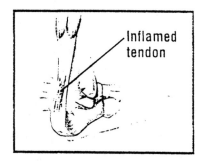
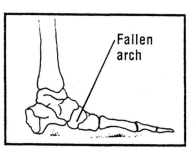
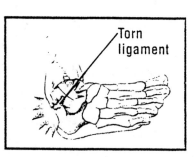

Figure 21. Types of Foot Problems.

Tendonitis:

Overuse can cause the tendons in the heel and the bottom of the foot to become inflamed. This leads to pain and swelling.

Ankle Sprains:

Sudden sideways movements can tear the ligaments in the ankle. This causes swelling, bruising, and pain.

Flat Feet:

Weak leg and foot muscles can cause the arch to collapse or fall. This leads to foot and leg pain, fatigue, and other problems.

What Causes Strains and Sprains?

Strains and sprains are caused when a joint is forced beyond its normal range of motion, or when muscles that are out of shape or haven't been warmed up properly are overworked. Back strain can occur with a sudden twist of the back or a lift without bending the knees.

Strains:

A strain occurs when a muscle or tendon is overstretched. Strains are usually caused by putting stress on tight or weak muscles.

Sprains:

A sprain is a tear in the ligament. Sprains are caused by the sudden, forceful twisting of a joint. If the tissue doesn't heal properly, the muscles may shorten.

This causes the joint to misalign and the nerves to become chronically irritated.

Tendonitis:

A tendon is a fibrous cord that attaches muscle to bone. Tendons often must go around sharp corners, through narrow spaces, and are in contact with other points of high wear. Generally there is a bursa, which lubricates the sliding tendon, decreasing the wear present. It may be at one of these joints that bursitis develops, or a condition known as tendonitis may occur.

Tendonitis is inflammation of a tendon. The same basic principles indicated previously in reference to bursitis are present in tendonitis. The only major differences are the tissue involved, the sliding activity of the tendon, and the locations within the body. The same thorough evaluation for the cause of tendonitis is very important in eliminating the condition rather than just overriding its symptoms.

Nervous System:

The nervous system is the body's communication network. Nerves run throughout the body, carrying messages though the spinal cord to the brain—the body's control center.

The brain receives information about the outside world from the nerves. It sorts the information and decides how the body should respond. Information travels along nerve fibers as electrical signals. This information is gathered from all over the body by sense organs—skin, tongue, nose, eyes, and ears.

The brain is made up of three main parts—the brainstem, the cerebellum, and the cerebrum. The brainstem controls involuntary actions, such as the heartbeat and breathing. The cerebellum coordinates movements of the muscles so that walking is smooth and balanced. The cerebrum is the largest part of the brain and is divided into two halves or hemispheres.

The outer layer of the cerebrum is a special area that receives messages about sight, touch, hearing, and taste while other areas control movement, intelligence, and personality.

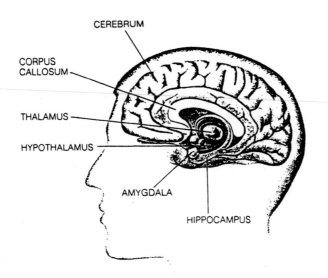

Figure 22. The Brain's Communication Network.

Nerve Root Problems:

With nerve root problems, the spinal nerves that pass through the vertebrae in the neck can become stretched, inflamed, or pinched. Workers may experience sharp pain shooting down their arms (often triggered by turning their head), or tingling, weakness, and numbness in the arms and hands. A nerve root problem can be caused by a variety of joint and disc problems, such as facet problems, a ruptured disc, or severe osteoarthritis. Left untreated, further neck or nerve problems can develop.

What Makes the Hands so Flexible?

The human hand is so sensitive that it can perform brain surgery, so strong that it can twist a screw deep into wood. Underlying the palm are the five cylinder-shaped metacarpal bones, which extend from the wrist to the knuckles. From the metacarpals rise the finger bones—the 14 jointed, flexible phalanges. In all, there are 27 bones in each hand. The bridge between hand and forearm is the wrist, a collection of eight small bones fitted together like cobblestones. These "carpal bones" are bound together in a glovelike structure of strong ligaments.

Fingers are controlled primarily by strong muscles in the forearm. These muscles connect with tendons, which are, on the palm side, embedded in long sheaths that extend along each finger. When the forearm muscle contracts, it tugs on the tendon and its sheath, and the finger bends. The thumb contributes to the hand's flexibility because it is opposed to the other fingers, which means one can easily pinch a small object between thumb and finger and pick it up.

Understanding Carpal Tunnel Syndrome (CTS):

Carpal Tunnel Syndrome is a common and troublesome condition that interferes with the use of the hand. It is caused when too much pressure is put on the nerve that runs through the wrist. A variety of anatomical abnormalities may be responsible for this vise-like pressure. Once symptoms of pain and tingling appear, the condition frequently worsens and permanent nerve damage may occur. However, CTS is highly treatable if diagnosed early.

Progressive Pain and Numbness:

The pain, numbness, and tingling of CTS can happen anywhere and anytime, at home or at work. But most often symptoms will first appear by waking the worker up at night. Shaking or massaging the hand may work temporarily, but if ignored, CTS gets progressively worse. The pain increases, the grip weakens, and workers may begin dropping things. Fortunately, appropriate treatment is available.

Take Action Early:

It's always best to prevent a condition, and CTS is no exception. But if your employees notice symptoms, don't wait for them to become unbearable. The earlier you recommend a professional diagnosis and treatment, the more successful the safety management outcome will be.

Senses and Ergonomics:

Three of the body's most important senses are sight, hearing, and sensation. The eyes and ears receive messages from the outside world and transmit them to the brain. It is critically important to understand how the senses work in order to accommodate for them.

The eye receives light rays that are reflected from an object. Light passes through the pupil and is focused by the cornea and lens. An upside-down picture is formed in the retina. Cells on the retina can sense light and color. These cells turn the picture into electrical signals that travel along the optic nerve to the brain. The brain then decodes the electrical signals, seeing the object the right side up.

Vision:

The way that our eyes and brain work together to produce images is incredibly sophisticated. Imagine building a robot that could follow a tiny baseball, hit it at 100 miles (60 km) per hour into the air, and run across a field to make a one-handed catch. The robot would need at least two eyes to see in three dimensions to judge the distance to the ball. But most important of all would be the robot's brain—the computer that interprets the images that the eyes create. When it comes to recognizing image, the human brain is still far more powerful than even the most powerful computers.

The human eye is a tough ball, filled with fluid, sitting in a bony socket. The cornea is the transparent, protective surface of the eye. It also focuses light. The iris controls the amount of light passing through the pupil. It closes up the pupil in bright light and opens it wide in dim light. The lens helps focus light on the retina, which contains a layer of light-sensitive cells. These send signals via the optic nerve to the brain, where they are interpreted to build up our view of the world.

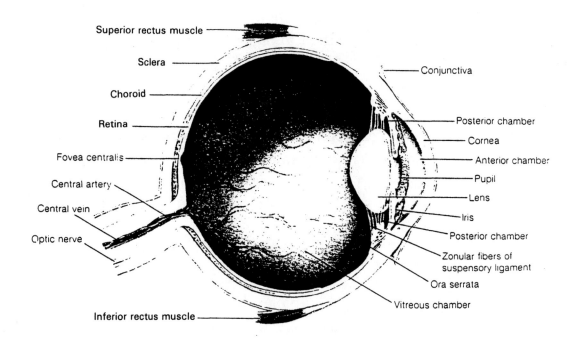

Figure 23. Structure of the Eye.

The Ear:

The ear collects waves of sound in the air. Sound waves pass along the auditory canal to the eardrum, making the thin skin of the eardrum vibrate. These vibrations travel through three tiny bones. They are then turned into electrical signals, which travel along the auditory nerve to the brain to interpret them as sound.

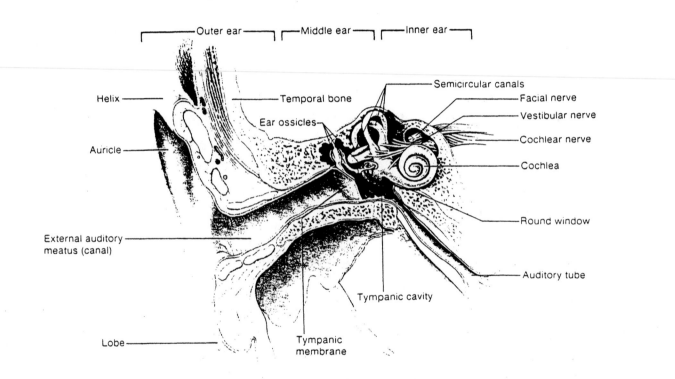

Figure 24. Structure of the Ear.

Measuring Sound:

Sounds can be loud or quiet, high-pitched (like a whistle), or low-pitched (like a truck engine.) Some sounds are pleasant; others are annoying or even painful.

But what makes one sound different from another? It has nothing to do with speed. All sounds travel at the same speed. If sounds did travel at different speeds, the sounds of instruments in an orchestra would reach your ears at different times and the music would be jumbled. The answer is that different sounds have different shaped waves. The feature of a sound wave that makes it quiet or loud is called its amplitude. The feature that makes the sound high-pitched or low-pitched is called the frequency. The wavelength—the distance between two wave compressions (crests)—also affects the sound.

Loudness:

The loudness of a sound depends on the intensity (amount of energy) carried by the sound waves. Big vibrations produce intense sound waves with large amplitudes. Very loud sounds, such as sonic booms and shock waves from explosions, can be painful and sometimes cause a lot of damage—the sound waves bang into structures and cause them to vibrate. A special scale called the decibel measures the loudness of sound.

Making and Hearing Sound:

If you have ever lost your voice, you know how difficult it is to make people understand you without it. Speech is our main form of communication. When we speak, we produce vibrations that travel through the air as sound waves. These sound waves are changed into sounds we can recognize with our ears. Although our ears can detect sounds in the range of 20 to 20,000 Hz, they are most sensitive to sounds with frequencies of around 1,000 Hz. This is the frequency range of voices in normal conversation, although our voices can produce sounds as low-pitched at 50 Hz and as high-pitched as 10,000 Hz. Just as we use our voices to talk to people, animals use sounds to communicate with each other.

Skin:

The human body is covered with an elastic layer called skin. Skin peforms many important jobs like holding the body together, keeping water and salts from seeping out of the body, and keeping harmful substances from getting in. The skin also senses touch and temperature.

Skin varies in thickness. It is nearly six times thicker on the soles of the feet than it is on the eyelids.

Skin varies in form, too. The skin around the elbows and knees is loose to allow them bend. The skin on the palm of the hand is firm and ridged so that it can grip.

Look at your fingertips under a magnifying glass and you will see that they have a pattern of ridges. These are your own unique set of fingerprints. The ridges are formed before you are born and no one else has the same pattern.

The skin is made up of different layers. The outside of the skin, called the epidermis, is a layer of flat, dead cells. These cells contain keratin to make the skin waterproof and tough. The cells are constantly being worn away, but they are replaced by new cells, which move toward the surface and harden. Other cells produce a special pigment called melanin. Melanin darkens the skin and protects it from strong sunlight.

Under the epidermis is a thicker, more elastic layer called the dermis. Here, sebaceous glands produce an oily substance, which helps keep the skin and hair soft and waterproof. Thread-like nerves can sense pain, touch, temperature, and pressure. Blood vessels, hair follicles, and sweat glands all help control body temperature.

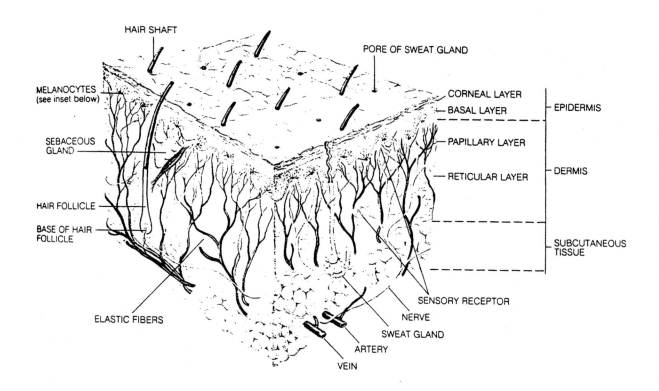

Figure 25. Structure of the Skin.

When the body is too hot, blood vessels widen, bringing more warm blood nearer the skin's surface. The air outside cools the blood. Sweat glands produce moisture, which dries on the skin to cool down the body.

When the body is cold, the blood vessels narrow. Goose pimples form when tiny muscles contract to push hairs up on end to trap the warm air next to the skin.

Beneath the dermis is a layer of fat that helps keep the body warm and stores energy.

Special Considerations in Ergonomics and the Body:

Water:

Maintain access to water for all employees. About two-thirds of the body is water and this level must be balanced. The body takes in 2.5 quarts of water a day through food and drink. It loses about 0.5 quarts of water breathing and 1.5 to 2 quarts through urination. Glands control the water balance in the body.

Quality Air—Respiration:

The energy contained in food is converted into energy used by a chemical reaction called respiration. This reaction is carried out in every single cell of the body and in nearly all living cells in the world. There are two kinds of respiration: aerobic and anaerobic. Aerobic respiration requires oxygen. It releases a great deal of energy.

Breathing:

The lungs supply the body with oxygen gas by breathing in air. Without oxygen, most body cells would only live for a few minutes. Cells use oxygen to break down food into energy, carbon dioxide gas, and water. By breathing out, the lungs remove carbon dioxide and water. This is called respiration.

When we breathe in, air is drawn in through the nose and mouth and travels down a large tube called the windpipe. The windpipe divides into two bronchi, one going to each lung. Air passes through these and then through a series of smaller and smaller tubes which end in tiny air sacs called alveoli. Each alveolus is surrounded by small blood vessels. Oxygen from the air seeps through the walls of the alveoli into the blood. The oxygen is picked up by red blood cells and carried throughout the body.

When we breathe, the chest and ribs move in and out. This movement is controlled by a sheet of muscle called the diaphragm. To breathe in, the diaphragm contracts and moves down and air rushes into the lungs. To breathe out, the diaphragm relaxes and moves up, forcing air out of the lungs.

Designing and Disease

Advances in medicine and technology have created the need for environments to support people with diseases through longer periods of life expectancy. A person with heart disease (the third most frequent disease in America), for instance, can live an average of seven more years after triple by-pass surgery. The ergonomic supports for this disease are those which provide comfort (posture and positioning, temperature control, access, and air quality). In the near future, people who are on dialysis machines may be receiving treatments at the work site. This will require quiet rooms with specialized technical supports. Awareness of these impending needs allows managers planning to use benchmark specifications from the health care industry to reconsider the traditional design of work areas. To illustrate the range of ergonomic needs for which safety managers may be called upon to accommodate, Table 1 is shown.

Designing and Injury

Today, workers' compensation is one of the most difficult costs for an organization to control. To understand, evaluate, and incorporate design strategies into a management plan is to sustain a competitive edge in a unique manner. For example, supporting maintenance functions with ergonomic designs would reduce the risk of injury in one of the most frequent injury categories. Have you ever tried to change a filter on a heating, ventilation, and air conditioning (HVAC) system? The posture requirements of such a task could challenge a Yogi.

Table 1. 1990 Census Data (In Thousands)

Functional Limitation	Total	Males				Females			
		Under 18	18-44	45-69	70-84	Under 18	18-44	45-69	70-84
Difficulty Interpretting Information	2,722	492	283	363	311	241	220	311	340
Limitation of Sight	4,509	146	532	833	342	118	403	1,148	731
Total Blindness	396	14	45	72	53	4	27	43	78
Limitation of Hearing	1,077	223	184	131	66	153	124	117	66
Total Deafness	1,700	80	80	452	307	80	80	205	243
Limitation of Speech	4,442	563	325	909	640	365	284	584	570
Susceptibility to Fainting, Dizziness, or Seizures	13,298	262	821	3,510	1,232	210	1,079	4,057	1,780
Incoordination	6,513	648	1,430	1,108	450	374	827	921	617
Limitation of Stamina	19,176	853	1,404	4,766	1,766	627	1,853	5,299	2,150
Limitation of Head Movement	12,680	150	1,690	2,312	569	179	1,342	3,367	1,619
Limitation of Sensation	4,887	60	859	1,193	221	37	616	1,367	459
Difficulty in Lifting and Reaching with Arms	12,281	192	1,803	2,544	714	159	1,595	4,001	1,771
Difficulty in Handling and Fingering	10,278	598	1,295	1,952	632	315	1,066	3,281	1,661
Inability to Use Upper Extremities	328	4	84	105	26	9	26	46	20
Difficulty in Sitting	13,146	168	1,815	2,440	574	192	1,420	3,480	1,632
Difficulty in Using Lower Extremities	18,031	317	2,358	3,446	1,134	324	2,181	5,203	2,628
Poor Balance	11,211	248	1,313	1,921	681	218	1,208	3,374	1,879

Summary — A Factor Analysis Approach to Safety Management and Ergonomics

This section was presented as a systematic review of the design and human factors that should be considered in creating productive and safe environments. The factors support the productive, efficient, and safe use of space. The understanding and organization of these factors is meant to allow you to "study the elephant one part at a time." However, the ultimate goal is to understand the factors as part of a matrix of factors that continuously interact with one another. In other words, no one factor stands alone. "Even though we're looking at big ears, IT'S STILL AN ELEPHANT."

The Design Factors

ACCESSIBILITY
ADAPTABILITY
AIR QUALITY
BENCHMARKING
COMFORT
COMMUNICATION
COST
   EFFECTIVENESS
DENSITY
DESIGN
DIVISION OF SPACE
ENERGY

EQUIPMENT/
   CONTROLS
FINISHES
FURNISHINGS
IMAGE
LANDSCAPING
LIGHTING
MAINTENANCE–
   INTERIOR
MATERIAL
   RESOURCE
   CONSERVATION

NOISE
PASSAGES
PLANNING
SAFETY
SECURITY
SIGNAGE
STORAGE
TEMPERATURE
TOOLS
WINDOWS

Section 1

Accessibility

```
┌─────────────────────────────────────────────────────────────────┐
│                   Human Factors to Be Considered                  │
│                                                                   │
│   Biomechanical :                    Sensory:                     │
│      ☐  Balance                         ☐   Vision                │
│      ☐  Coordination                    ☐   Hearing               │
│      ☐  Sitting                         ☐   Olfactory             │
│      ☐  Standing                        ☐   Speech                │
│      ☐  Head Movement                   ☐   Skin                  │
│      ☐  Lifting/Reaching             Psychological:               │
│      ☐  Handling and Fingering          ☐   Stress - Fatigue      │
│      ☐  Use of Upper Extremities     Intellectual:                │
│      ☐  Use of Lower Extremities        ☐   Coordination          │
│      ☐  Stamina                         ☐   Concentration         │
└─────────────────────────────────────────────────────────────────┘
```

The importance of accessibility in ergonomics is to consider the optimum locations of both static work components (e.g., bookshelves, large machines) and dynamic work components (e.g., controls, seating, materials). Accessibility to these components should be considered when they are used by individuals to perform tasks. The objective of ergonomic accessiility is to evaluate each component's accessibility relative to the unique human factor needs of the individuals or groups using that component. Biomechanical needs should be considered based on the position a person must assume to effectively be mobile within a space, manipulate objects and equipment, and participate in work-related activities. For example, components should be arranged in a workspace by frequency of use—with the most frequently used components within the easiest reach. Sensory needs should also be considered in order to accommodate eye-hand interaction. Psychological needs should be considered to support productivity and safety. Additionally, components that are organized by function are less stressful. For example, all components used for quality testing on a single product should be accessible on the same workbench. Intellectual needs should be considered to support productivity and quality by creating access to components in the optimum sequence of use and by importance. For example, assembly parts organized in a left to right semi-circle are arranged in a familiar pattern. Accessibility is the optimum location of work components in relation to the employee performing the tasks.

1.1 Ergonomic Design Benefits

- ☐ Improved design

- ☐ Improved safety

- ☐ Legal compliance

1.2 Consequences of Not Using Ergonomic Design

- ☐ Lost time

- ☐ Increased cost

- ☐ Legal citation

- ☐ Injury, illness

- ☐ Disease

- ☐ Fatality

- ☐ Lost quality

1.3   Importance of Accessibility

☐   People spend 70% of their workday in their work area, typically at their workstation moving within a 3 to 5 foot radius.

☐   People with an assigned work area typically spend 30% of their time away from their work area (10% in another person's area, 27% resourcing their tasks, 18% in conference rooms, and 45% off their floor of location.)

1.4   Accessibility Guidelines

☐   Orient the work area so that the employee can face the work without twisting, turning, or bending.

☐   Make sure the work surface height accommodates work type and visual requirements.

Work type	Work Surface *(In reference to elbow height)*
Delicate/fine work, writing, assembly	2-4 inches above
General handwork	2-4 inches below
Manual work, using tools	4-6 inches below
Heavy manual work using upper back/legs.	6-16 inches below

☐   Angle the work surface to enhance visual acuity.

☐   Build in adjustability. If unable to adjust, then design according to population percentiles:

-   Establish work surface height for 50th to 95th percentile worker.
-   Establish reaches and shelf/conveyer heights for 5th percentile female (smallest worker).

☐   Orient all incoming/outgoing products and materials for easy access in (correct angle) and to (correct height).

☐   All side movements should be down and out, within 14-18 reach, and at working height or slightly below.

☐   Design areas so that movement occurs in the same horizontal plane

-   All objects to be manipulated should be arranged so that the most frequent movements occur with the elbows bent and close to the sides.

☐   For optimal hand/arm strength and skill, work should be placed 10-12 inches in front of eyes, and elbows should be bent at an 85-100° angle.

☐   If objects need to be higher and closer for visual acuity, use supports under them. These supports should be padded and adjustable.

Section 2

Adaptability

```
┌─────────────────────────────────────────────────────────────┐
│              Human Factors to Be Considered                   │
│                                                               │
│  Biomechanical :                    Sensory:                  │
│     ☐  Balance                         ☐  Vision              │
│     ☐  Coordination                    ☐  Hearing             │
│     ☐  Sitting                         ☐  Olfactory           │
│     ☐  Standing                        ☐  Speech              │
│     ☐  Head Movement                   ☐  Skin                │
│     ☐  Lifting/Reaching             Psychological:            │
│     ☐  Handling and Fingering          ☐  Stress - Fatigue    │
│     ☐  Use of Upper Extremities     Intellectual:             │
│     ☐  Use of Lower Extremities        ☐  Coordination        │
│     ☐  Stamina                         ☐  Concentration       │
│                                                               │
└─────────────────────────────────────────────────────────────┘
```

The importance of adaptability in ergonomics is to consider the optimum flexibility of the components of work as they relate to both the structural dimensions of the body (such as height and weight) and the functional dimensions of the body (such as reach or mobility). Adaptability is determined by evaluating the relationship between the flexibility of components in a space to the widest range of human capabilities within that space. An example of biomechanical adaptability is the ability to raise or lower the height of a work surface to meet the needs of people whose torsos range from 30 inches to 45 inches. An example of sensory adaptability is the ability to control lighting in a room. An example of intellectual adaptability is the ability to design and redesign the sequence of movements, given the limitations of piece of equipment.

Adaptability provides for the optimum flexibility of of workplace components for employees.

2.1 Ergonomic Design Benefits

☐ Improved productivity

☐ Improved safety

☐ Legal compliance

2.2 Consequences of Not Using Ergonomic Design

☐ Lost time

☐ Increased cost

☐ Poor quality

2.3 Importance of Adaptability

☐ Technology continues to enhance human capability.

☐ Changing environments and personal needs due to aging, injury, disease, and disability are critical to adaptability.

2.4 Ergonomic Adaptability

☐ Design work areas, surfaces, and tools with technologies that are integrated into other key design factors and that satisfy the expectations of *both the supervisor and the employee.*

☐ Employers need to know if the work site design makes the best use of the following:

- esthetics and image
- ease of maintenance
- function and fitness
- lowered first costs and life cycle costs
- responsiveness of a status marking system
- bulk purchase agreements or existing inventory

☐ Employers need to know if the room satisfies the following criteria while meeting corporate standards, laws, and guidelines:

- appearance
- comfort
- ease of communication
- ease of participation
- flexibility
- layout
- occupancy level
- relocation frequency
- safety (rules posted)
- grounded equipment
- no extension cords

- safe smoking areas
- secure rugs

☐ Both employees and employers need to know if the room provides an atmosphere that does the following:

- increases opportunities for individual choice
- encourages independence
- compensates for changes in perception and sensory acuity
- decreases unnecessary mobility
- encourages social interaction
- stimulates participation in activities offered
- reduces conflict and distraction
- provides a safe environment
- makes activities accessible
- improves employer and employee image
- allows for growth and change in individuals

2.5   Design Recommendations

Taking into consideration the environmental design and specific individual design factors of work environments, work stations and work technologies are uniquely designed for individual capabilities. These quality check recommendations illustrate the range of customized options that increase productivity while reducing stress and fatigue.

☐ Are tasks performed more efficiently?

☐ Are productivity rates maintained or exceeded?

☐   Are stressors diminished?

☐   Have muscular stressors been eliminated?

☐   Have injuries and symptoms been reduced?

☐   Is the physical relationship with equipment well integrated for the employee?

☐   Are accessories within easy reach?

☐   Are there resources for doing the tasks?

☐   Has the intensity of concentration required been reduced?

☐   Is the environment totally accessible?

☐   Have the individual's limitations been mitigated by well-integrated interventions?

☐   What effect have the interventions had on other employees and supervisors?

Section 3

Air Quality

```
┌────────────────────────────────────────────────────────────────────┐
│                    Human Factors to Be Considered                    │
│                                                                      │
│   Biomechanical :                        Sensory:                    │
│      ☐  Balance                             ☐  Vision                │
│      ☐  Coordination                        ☐  Hearing               │
│      ☐  Sitting                             ☐  Olfactory             │
│      ☐  Standing                            ☐  Speech                │
│      ☐  Head Movement                       ☐  Skin                  │
│      ☐  Lifting/Reaching                 Psychological:              │
│      ☐  Handling and Fingering              ☐  Stress - Fatigue      │
│      ☐  Use of Upper Extremities         Intellectual:               │
│      ☐  Use of Lower Extremities            ☐  Coordination          │
│      ☐  Stamina                             ☐  Concentration         │
│                                                                      │
└────────────────────────────────────────────────────────────────────┘
```

The importance of air quality in ergonomics is to consider the optimum air purity for unique individuals and groups in the workplace environment. The difficulty in maintaining air quality is the range of human responses to air contaminants that may or may not be regulated by OSHA exposure limits but nevertheless cause physiological reactions. Increasingly, individuals in work environments are complaining of reactions to perfumes, secondary smoke, off-gases from copying machines, etc. Some common physiological reactions include runny nose, itchy eyes, and headaches. Therefore, an ergonomic evaluation needs to go beyond regulated air pollutants such as smoke, exhaust fumes, toxic vapors, gases, insecticides, herbicides, and ionizing radiation and consider "discomfort" as a valid indicator of the need to investigate and resoluve air quality concerns. The question then becomes what degree of concentration and exposure time to what "pollutants" is an acceptable exposure.

3.1   Ergonomic Design Benefits

☐   Increased fresh air

☐   Improved comfort

☐   Improved safety

☐   Legal compliance

3.2   Consequences of Not Using Ergonomic Design

☐   Lost time

☐   Increased cost of energy

☐   System failures

☐   Legal citations

☐   Injury, illness

☐   Disease

☐   Fatality

☐   Lost quality

3.3   Air Quality and Ergonomic Design

☐   Employees need the following:

-    increased exposure and access to outdoor landscaped spaces
-    clear views with season and time of day indications
-    natural ventilation with the effective distribution of fresh air

☐   Safety managers must review air distribution and exhaust and the selection of enclosure materials to reduce outgassing and unwanted moisture migration (with resulting condensation and bacterial growth.)

☐   In addition, review:

-    operable windows, linkages, air intakes, and exhausts
-    cross ventilation with side, top, or filtered openings
-    roof monitors, stack, and suction ventilation
-    mechanically assisted ventilation
-    displacement ventilation
-    night ventilation, flywheel effect
-    access to outdoor work and break areas

3.4   Ergonomics and Defining Fresh Air Architecture

A wide range of approaches to providing healthier air quality in workplaces has been demonstrated in Japan, Germany, North America, the U.K., and France. The air quality approaches ranging from innovations in building systems to innovations in operational attitudes.

3.5 Eight Major Categories of Innovation Deemed Critical to the Emerging Definition of Fresh Air Architecture

☐ Innovative heating, ventilation, and air quality (HVAC) system designs

☐ Maximized individual control of environmental systems

☐ Increased outside environmental contact for the individual

☐ Effective pollution source control

☐ Demonstration of concern for the environment and building resource management

☐ Demonstration of concern for the effectiveness of the building systems

☐ Demonstration of concern for the health, comfort, and satisfaction of the occupants

☐ Relationship of air quality to productivity

3.6 Factors Affecting Indoor Air Quality

☐ There are four factors that affect indoor air quality:

- HVAC systems
- interior and exterior pollutant or contaminant sources
- pollutant pathway

- building occupants

Table 3-1. Houseplants and Their Influence on Airborne Microbes		
	Plant Filled Sunroom (Mean Values)	Bedroom Free of Houseplants (Mean Values)
Airborne Microbes (cfu/4-hours)	4.44 (± 0.06)	12.76 (± 3.94)
Temperature (°F)	72.22 (± 2.20)	72.68 (± 1.74)
Relative Humidity (%)	72.18 (± 2.09)	56.54 (± 2.77)

☐ Indoor air should not contain contaminants that reach or exceed concentrations known to impair health or cause discomfort to building occupants. Such contaminants include:

- various gases, vapors
- microorganisms
- smoke
- other particulate matters

These contaminants may be present already in outside air or be introduced from indoor activities, furnishings, building materials, surface coatings, or air handling and air treatment components.

3.6.1 Indoor Contaminants

☐ Existing contaminants must be maintained below the following levels:

Asbestos	< .01 fibers/cm^3
CO_2	< 1000 ppm
CO	< 35ppm
Formaldehyde	< .1ppm
Lead Dust or Fumes	< .15mg/m^3
Nitrogen Dioxide	< 3ppm
Radon	< 4pc/liter
Sulfur Dioxide	< 2ppm
Particulate	< 10mg/m^3
Tobacco Smoke	< .1mg/m^3
Penicillin	< 500cfu/m^3
Cladosporium	< 500cfu/m^3

☐ Building occupants play a major role in maintaining air quality. Air contaminants are introduced into the air by:

- perfume
- tobacco smoke
- personal hygiene products
- foods
- plants and pesticides
- copy machines
- office supplies
- some work-related activities
- other non-work activities

☐ Air movement and heating, ventilation, and air conditioning loads are affected by the presence of electronic equipment, by furniture design, and by space layout.

☐ HVAC control is affected by adjusting thermostats and ducts.

Based upon this information, the Federal Division of Buildings and Policy Services developed a comprehensive program to ensure that each building's air quality meets the requirements of safety and comfort, while maintaining effiecient energy use. The building management and staff recommendations included the following:

☐ Conduct periodic CO_2, humidity, and temperature testing to ensure comfort and safety.

☐ Install computerized building management systems to efficiently maintain and monitor HVAC control.

☐ Develop an automated preventive maintenance work order system to ensure efficient HVAC operation.

☐ Periodically evaluate and adjusting HVAC air balance for proper air movement.

3.7   Healthier Enclosure Design for the Workplace

Maximize environmental contact by:

☐ Increasing periphery and eliminating buried high-use spaces.

☐ Installing high visibility transmission glass.

☐ Allowing for direct access to the outside, with outside work/meeting/eating areas.

3.7.1 Design Provisions

☐ Layered, dynamic envelope provisions include:

- solar load control with exterior shading devices
- light and glare control with interior shading devices
- heat loss gain/control; high R-value facades and roofs
- low balancing with water mullion system

☐ Passive air conditioning provisions include:

- daylighting (with ambient and task control)
- natural ventilation (cross, stack and fan assist with PV)
- passive solar heating potential in low interior load conditions

☐ Air freshness provisions include:

- dedicated 20cfm outside air
- air supply independent of thermal demand
- operable windows for natural ventilation (a 5-minute purge cycle)
- air quality filters on supply side, distributed for access
- steam humidification on air side; ultrasonic individual units on water side

☐   Negotiated control provisions include:

-    individually controlled air speed, temperature, direction, OA content, and MRT
-    thermal energy monitoring, including individual "odometers"

☐   Passive and active ventilation provisions

ABCIS urges that the responsibility of the enclosure for ensuring a healthy building (real and perceived) be dependent on a series of architectural decisions, including:

-    increasing exposure and access to outdoor landscaped spaces
-    providing clear views with season and time of day indications
-    allowing natural ventilation, with the effective distribution of fresh air and removal of exhaust air
-    selecting enclosure materials that reduce outgassing and unwanted moisture migration (with the resulting condensation and bacterial growth)
    - operable windows, linkages, air intakes and exhausts
    - cross ventilation with side, top or filtered openings
    - roof monitors, stack and suction ventilation
    - mechanically-assisted ventilation
    - displacement ventilation
    - night ventilation, flywheel effect
    - access to outdoor work and break areas;
-    gardens with non-polluted air, sun, wind, vegetation for shading, air purification and humidification, and water management

3.7.2 Ventilation

☐ Natural ventilation and its integration with the mechanical system may be the hardest to engineer, quantify, and integrate into the modern office.

☐ Natural ventilation in office environments requires pressure differences for cross ventilation and suction ventilation, or temperature differences for stack ventilation, to create a natural air movement through the workplace.

☐ Displacement ventilation relies on the natural horizontal migration of slightly cooler air to provide for the fresh air ventilation needs of the workplace (not the cooling needs).

☐ Night ventilation relies on the lower nighttime air temperatures to cool down the mass in the building's structure (concrete slabs for example), to provide an effective heat sink for the internal gain buildup the following day.

☐ Care must be taken not to overcool the building mass below dew point so that no condensation and potential bacterial growth can occur.

Section 4

Benchmarking

Human Factors to Be Considered

Biomechanical :
- ☐ Balance
- ☐ Coordination
- ☐ Sitting
- ☐ Standing
- ☐ Head Movement
- ☐ Lifting/Reaching
- ☐ Handling and Fingering
- ☐ Use of Upper Extremities
- ☐ Use of Lower Extremities
- ☐ Stamina

Sensory:
- ☐ Vision
- ☐ Hearing
- ☐ Olfactory
- ☐ Speech
- ☐ Skin

Psychological:
- ☐ Stress - Fatigue

Intellectual:
- ☐ Coordination
- ☐ Concentration

Benchmarking describes the practice of comparing products, services, and methods with those of other organizations and companies known to be leaders in their fields. The objective of benchmarking is to identify and adapt the leaders' best practices or procedures. Understanding benchmarking provides a competitive edge while creating a safer and healthier environment based on the highest quality practices.

4.1   Ergonomic Design Benefits

- ☐   Legal compliance

- ☐   Improved comfort

☐   Improved safety

4.2   Consequences of Not Using Ergonomic Design

☐   Lost time

☐   Increased cost of energy

☐   System failures

☐   Legal citations

☐   Injury, illness

☐   Disease

☐   Fatality

☐   Lost quality

4.3   Importance of Benchmarking

☐   Benchmark areas may include:

      - cost of worker's compensation
      - cost of occupational health nurse
      - cost of ergonomic assessment

4.3.1 Possible Areas for Benchmarking

☐   Extent of training programs' success

☐   Use of computerized maintenance programs

☐   Size of offices or workspace cubicles

☐   CAD utilization

☐   Food services

☐   Furniture inventory

☐   Landscape, flooring, and asphalt maintenance

☐   Use of blanket purchase orders

☐   Staff size

☐   Cost per square foot for construction/remodelling for safety

☐   Safety

☐   Use of JIT inventory on material handling

☐   Churn rates

4.3.2 Areas of Interaction

☐ Headcount

☐ Environmental responsibilities

☐ Gross square footage occupied

☐ FM ergonomic budgets

☐ Ownership of space

☐ Charging for space and services

☐ Vacancy rate of space

☐ Contracting services

☐ Churn rate

☐ Use of computer applications

☐ Space allocation policies

☐ Storage of graphic assessment information

4.3.3 Structure of the Safety Department

☐ Use of performance indicators

☐ Reporting structure

☐ Communication with building users' current property issues

4.4 Suggested Tasks for Implementation of a Benchmarking Study

☐ Establish a local benchmarking group of safety managers with other companies or other institutions of similar mix and size.

☐ Participate in the American Society of Safety Engineers (ASSE) national benchmarking process, and others as appropriate.

☐ Receive periodic (at least annual) benchmarking comparative reports from the safety council group.

☐ Create ongoing focus groups of the participating companies, to share and implement ideas for continuous improvement.

☐ Encourage participation by all levels of the safety management organization.

4.4.1 Implementation

☐ Benchmarking is practiced by comparing one department within an organization to a similar department in a different corporation/ institution, no matter the type of industry. This is key to successful measurement.

4.5   The Measurement Process

Most organizations, especially those in manufacturing areas, have found ways to measure processes. Many companies have adopted specific ways of measuring—for example, Statistical Process Control (SPC). Identified below are some of the more common methods of measurement that could be applied to the facilities or organization to establish a measurement process in your organization.

4.5.1 General Measurement Processes

☐   Customer satisfaction surveys

☐   ISO 9000 requirements

☐   Baldrige steps

☐   Benchmarking

-    internal
-    external

☐   Matrices planning

☐   Statistical process control (SPC)

☐   Hoshin planning

☐   Value engineering (design)

☐   Earned process value

☐ Skills assessment

☐ Deming's 14 steps and 7 sins

☐ Quality functional deployment

☐ Total productive maintenance (TPM)

☐ Key driver determination

☐ Deming's plan/do/check/act (PDCA)

4.6 ISO 9000

In 1987, the International Organization for Standardization (ISO) adopted the ISO 9000 series quality system management standards. The major factor driving worldwide use of the standard is the unification of 12 major European nations into a single trading union called the European Economic Community.

4.6.1 ISO Standard Is a Two-Fold Opportunity

☐ ISO registration will soon be a European requirement.

☐ The discipline required for ISO 9000 enhances and improves existing quality systems, especially in written standards and procedures.

4.7 Areas of Interest in Ergonomic Planning

☐ Section 1.0—Management Responsibility

- Responsibilities, job descriptions, and qualifications are documented properly and available for review or audit within the department.

☐ Section 4.0—Document Control

- Documentation is authorized, dated, and signed with revision level control and history.

☐ Section 5.0—Purchasing

- Procedures for qualification and assessment of subcontractors are documented.

☐ Section 10.0—Inspection, Measuring, and Test Equipment

- All equipment used in facilities on the master Corporate Calibration List is inspected, measured, and tested.

☐ Section 12—Control of Non-Conforming Product

- Procedure for handling supplier non-conformance is documented.

☐ Section 13—Corrective Action

- Procedure for initiating, tracking, and following up on corrective actions is documented.

☐ Section 16—Internal Quality Audits

- Records of internal audits are maintained.

4.8 Quality Measures

☐ External image

☐ Worker satisfaction

☐ Supplier evaluation (recommended by ergonomists)

4.9 Financial Measures

☐ Accounts payable

☐ Budgets

☐ Revenue/square footage (return on investment)

4.10 Timeliness Measures

☐ Project delivery time

☐ Downtime

4.11 Productivity/Efficiency Measures

☐ Safety/security

☐ Teams of designers and technicians

☐ Information technology

☐ Worker utilization

☐ Innovation

☐ Education

☐ Planning

☐ Environmental practices

☐ Products and/or services

☐ Process for legal compliance

☐ Technology

☐ Organizational structure

☐ Historic growth, workers' compensation reduction trends

☐ Revenue per person or revenue per area

☐ Competition

☐ Problems with existing conditions

☐ Inventory distribution of ergonomic products

☐ Finance/accounting systems and methods

☐ External environments

4.12 Locations and their Components

☐ Locations—properties, sites, and buildings ownership/ lease data

- amount (gross, rentable, usable)
- classification of usage (category, type and standard)
- occupancy/ownership status
- physical condition and functional performance for corporate mission

☐ Primary systems

- foundations—substructure
- exterior closure
- roofing

☐ Secondary systems

- partitions and doors
- walls and furniture
- floor finishes
- ceiling finishes

☐ Service systems—conveying

- conveying for material handling

☐ Service systems—mechanical

- plumbing
- heating
- cooling
- lighting
- power

☐ Safety standards

☐ Energy conservation

☐ Handicapped access

☐ Functional standards

☐ Financial performance (operational costs)

☐ Legal restrictions

☐ Personnel access to safety services

- personnel identifiers
- position standard
- location
- telephone number
- organization unit
- activity

☐ Furniture/equipment recommendations

- open plan components (by standard)
- free standing units (by standard)
- large or expensive pieces
- requirements
- adjacencies

☐ Telecommunications

4.13 Goals for a Safety Project

Goals for a safety project must meet and comply with:

☐ Corporate vision

☐ Corporate audit

☐ Strategic and tactical plans

- the facility forecast
- corporate communication information
- how any of the following will effect the corporation

☐ Economic conditions

- national and international

☐ Demographics

- markets
- site locations

- labor pools

☐ Work force

- women
- minorities
- immigrants

4.14 Workforce Statistics

☐ By the year 2020, two-thirds of the American work force will be minority or female.

☐ In 1985, 47% of the work force was American-born, white-males; by 2000, this will dwindle to 15%.

☐ Immigrant men and women made up 7% of the work force in 1985 and are projected to represent 22% of the work force by 2000, increasing even higher in the later years.

☐ Women of all cultures will represent almost half of the work force by 2000.

☐ Over 600,000 immigrants will enter the country each year in the foreseeable future. This will affect the following:

- marketing and distribution of products
- financial policies
- telecommunications and computer needs
- expectations for employee welfare, health and safety policies

- physical environment and aesthetic of locations
- social, cultural, and educational opportunities in the workplace
- political trends
- ecological trends
- technological trends

4.15 Healthier Interior Design for the Workplace

☐ Design changes

- low outgassing and low-radiation materials (furniture, walls, carpets, fabrics, paints, adhesives)
- selection of recycled and recyclable materials
- renewable materials
- easily maintained materials
- high integrity materials

☐ Construction changes

- remote outgassing of delivered products
- reduced pollution "sinks" during construction
- direct outdoor exhaust continuous during construction
- no fast-track occupancy

☐ Operation changes

- dedicated exhaust at service hubs and relocatable office exhausts
- low-pollution products (computers, toners, cleaners)
- recycling of office products

- plants as filters, oxygenators and mood uplifters
- occupancy questionnaires
- complaint response
- diagnostic evaluations, embedded, robotics, transportable

Section 5

Comfort

```
┌─────────────────────────────────────────────────────────────┐
│              Human Factors to Be Considered                  │
│                                                              │
│  Biomechanical :                    Sensory:                 │
│     ☐  Balance                         ☐  Vision             │
│     ☐  Coordination                    ☐  Hearing            │
│     ☐  Sitting                         ☐  Olfactory          │
│     ☐  Standing                        ☐  Speech             │
│     ☐  Head Movement                   ☐  Skin               │
│     ☐  Lifting/Reaching             Psychological:           │
│     ☐  Handling and Fingering          ☐   Stress - Fatigue  │
│     ☐  Use of Upper Extremities     Intellectual:            │
│     ☐  Use of Lower Extremities        ☐  Coordination       │
│     ☐  Stamina                         ☐  Concentration      │
│                                                              │
└─────────────────────────────────────────────────────────────┘
```

The importance of comfort in ergonomics is to keep in mind this one truth: people are not "typical" or "average"—they come in different shapes and sizes, vary in age, come from a variety of different cultures, and are likely to have a range of diseases, disabilities, injuries, and physical considerations. With that truth in mind, ergonomic designs should allow employees to be comfortable while using equipment, tools, and materials. Seating, entries with key systems, and toilet facilities are also important comfort considerations.

5.1 Ergonomic Design Benefits

☐   Improved productivity

☐   Improved safety

☐ Legal compliance

5.2 Consequences of Not Using Ergonomic Design

☐ Lost time

☐ Legal citation

☐ Injury, illness

☐ Disease

☐ Fatality

☐ Lost quality

5.3 Increased Workers' Compensation Claims

	PERCENT (%) INCREASE
Back injuries	99.19%
Carpal Tunnel Syndrome	86.26%
Repetitive motion, cumulative trauma	76.21%
Work-related stress (psychological)	39.52%
Needle sticks or other puncture wounds	36.69%
Head injuries	35.08%
Heart problems	25.00%
RSD Syndrome (continuous pain)	19.76%
Exposure to toxicity/hazardous substances	17.34%
Asbestos exposure	8.47%
Lead exposure (lead-based paint, etc.)	3.23%

Lyme Disease   3.23%

Other   15.32%

5.4   Results of Muscles Working at Maximum Capacity

☐   Inflammation and injuries, which result in pain

☐   Swelling

☐   Diminished range of motion

5.5   Use of Telephones

5.5.1 Suggested Telephone Techniques and Purchases

☐   Use hand-held telephone.

☐   Alternate sides.

☐   Purchase a rest.

☐   Purchase a headset.

5.5.2 Caution

☐   Worker should always avoid holding the telephone receiver with the ear and shoulder.

5.6 Proper Chair Adjustments with Footrest

☐ Minimize muscle activity to maintain posture.

☐ Reduce disc pressure to spine.

☐ Maintain load bearing to the chair not the body.

5.7 Seating

☐ Adjust height to maintain feet flat on the floor.

☐ Incline back rest and seat angle.

☐ Provide back support to lumbar.

☐ Adjust armrests to support weight to the arms.

☐ Shorten seat pan to prevent pressure on veins in thighs.

☐ Fit seat pan to ischial.

5.8 Footrests

☐ Tilt angle adjusts knee angle to slightly above pelvis to aid circulation and reduce stress to the heart.

☐ Foot pedals decrease static load to the muscles of the legs and thighs.

☐   Flat platform adjusts knee angle or levels the foot for access.

☐   Warming pads reduce the discomfort of cold floors that can aid in such diseases as arthritis and post polio syndrome.

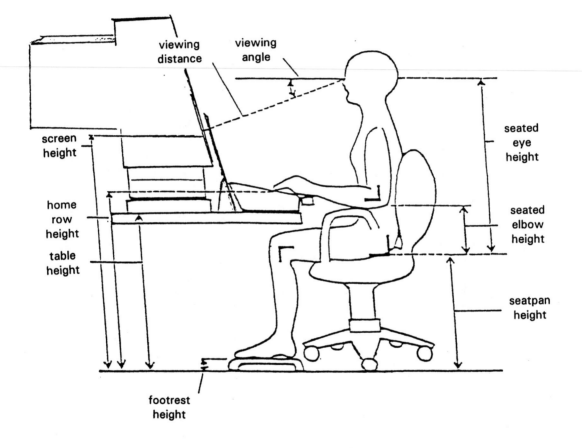

**Figure 5-1. Proper Ergonomic Seating Design for
Employee at Computer Terminal.**

5.9 Seating and Comfort

☐ Because of the uniqueness of each employee's body and the stresses on it due to hours of sitting, proper seating is one of the most important ergonomic interventions a safety manager provides.

☐ The goal of all ergonomic interventions is to maintain productivity and efficiency while reducing stress and fatigue. Proper seating therefore becomes one of the more difficult purchases.

5.9.1 Postural Supports

Seated postures require a minimum of five integrated postural supports:

☐ Feet to supported surface (footrest or floor) with wheel base and support cylinder.

☐ Legs, buttocks, and trunk support through seat pan and backrest.

☐ Lumbar spine support through seat pan and backrests' lumbar support.

☐ Shoulders and arms support through backrests and chair arm supports.

☐ Head and neck suppport through backrests and chair arm supports.

CHANGE IN POSTURE OF THE SPINE		NORMAL LUMBAR LORDOSIS BECOMES KYPHOSIS
LUMBAR DISC PRESSURE		SITTING CAUSES 35% INCREASED PRESSURE ON DISCS
BACK MUSCLE ACTIVITY		MUSCLE ACTIVITY DECREASED
'LACTIC ACID BUILDUP	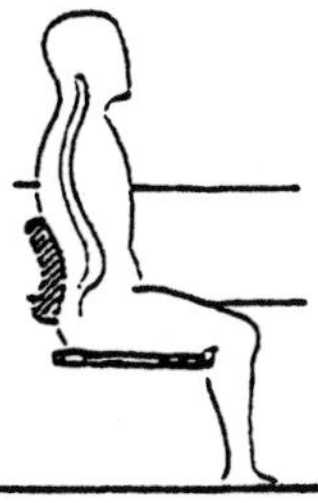	STATIC LOAD AT BACK OF LEG AND TRUNK DECREASED BLOOD FLOW FATIGUE AND PAIN
THIGH PRESSURE		VEIN COMPRESSION (HEART WORKS HARDER)
PRESSURE ON BUTTOCKS		85 TO 100 PSI ON ISCHIAL TUBEROSITIES (DOUBLE WITH LEGS CROSSED)

Figure 5-2. The Physical Stress of Sitting.

IMPROPER BODY POSTURES

CHAIR NOT ADJUSTED TO TASK

KNEE FLEXED TOO MUCH

WEIGHT OF BODY TO
ISCHIAL

PELVIS ROTATED

SPINE FLEXED

ORGANS COMPRESSED

FEET UNSUPPORTED

SLIDE FORWARD

AWKWARD REACH

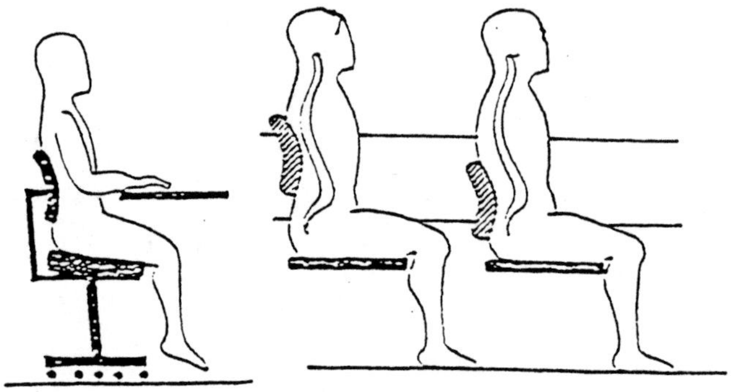

Feet
unsupported

Back rest
too high

Back rest
too low

Figure 5-3. Improper Body Postures Caused by Lack of Support.

5.9.2 Maintenance of Balance

☐ The height from the floor to the seat pan is critical for workers to integrate their bodies with their workstations, equipment, and materials.

☐ The back can work twice as hard maintaining posture when a seat is either too high or too low, in order to compensate for pelvic rotation. In addition, the maintenance of "safe movement" reduces the likelihood of over-reaching for materials.

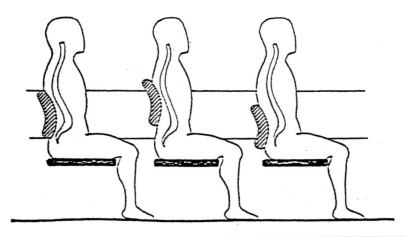

Figure 5-4. Maintenance of Balance.

☐ A minimum of 5 to 6 caster bases is recommended with breaking casters.

5.9.3 What Chairs Must Support

☐ Chairs must provide support that maintains the lumbar spine and pelvis in the naturally curved position.

- reduces pressure on the discs

☐ Lumbar supports must transfer the person's weight from the spine to the support.

- reduces disc compression and the possibility of injury and pain

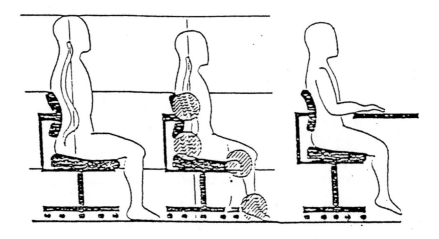

Figure 5-5. What Chairs Must Support.

5.9.4 Body Position

☐ Chairs must allow for changes in body position.

- reduces static load on the back and trunk
- reduces cause muscle fatigue and pain

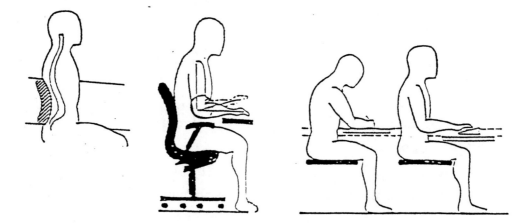

Figure 5-6. Body Support in Seated Positions.

☐   The employee must be able to adjust the chair's height to varying work surfaces.

☐   Forearm supports at the level of the work surface are needed.

-   reduces disc pressure and muscle strain

5.9.5 Seat Pan

☐   The seat pan of a chair must be flexible enough to allow for load changes and the compression of buttocks and thighs.

-   reduces pressure under the thigh
-   reduces stiffness
-   reduces the heart working harder to pump blood through the circulatory system

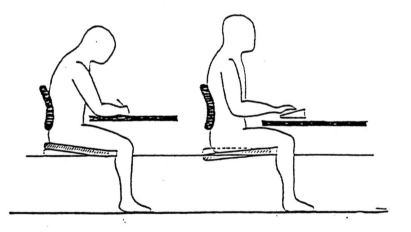

Figure 5-7. Importance of the Seat Pan.

5.9.6 Backrests

☐ Backrests must incline in tandem with the seat pan in order to promote the proper support of the body.

- reduces dependence on the muscles and spine
- helps to maintain good posture

5.9.7 Footrests

☐ Footrests should be used to take the pressure off the thighs and raise the knees above the level of the hips.

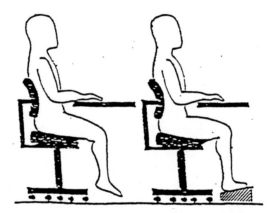

Figure 5-8. Support Provided by Footrest.

Section 6

Communication

```
┌─────────────────────────────────────────────────────────────────┐
│                  Human Factors to Be Considered                   │
│                                                                   │
│  Biomechanical :                        Sensory:                  │
│      ☐  Balance                            ☐  Vision              │
│      ☐  Coordination                       ☐  Hearing             │
│      ☐  Sitting                            ☐  Olfactory           │
│      ☐  Standing                           ☐  Speech              │
│      ☐  Head Movement                      ☐  Skin                │
│      ☐  Lifting/Reaching                Psychological:            │
│      ☐  Handling and Fingering             ☐  Stress - Fatigue    │
│      ☐  Use of Upper Extremities        Intellectual:            │
│      ☐  Use of Lower Extremities           ☐  Coordination        │
│      ☐  Stamina                            ☐  Concentration       │
└─────────────────────────────────────────────────────────────────┘
```

The ergonomic importance of communication in the workplace is to consider communication key to productivity, safety, and quality. While the means of communications continues to change—from speech and words on paper to beepers, faxes, phones, e-mail, answering machines, and digitized boards to name a few—the ergonomic initiative remains to categorize the means and the messages of communications and develop conditions that increase the favorability of speaking and listening conditions. Some suggested solutions include the use of quiet rooms, earphones, headsets, acoustical treatments, baffles on machines, and training talkers and listeners to accommodate their environments to their communication needs.

6.1 Ergonomic Design Benefits

☐ Improved productivity

☐ Improved safety

☐ Legal compliance

6.2 Consequences of Not Using Ergonomic Design

☐ Legal citation

☐ Injury, illness

☐ Disease

☐ Fatality

☐ Lost quality

6.3 Goals of Ergonomic Communication

☐ Maximize interaction.

☐ Encourage communication.

☐ Remove impediments to productivity.

☐ Provide convenient and comfortable work environments that optimize a person's time for conducting tasks.

☐   Encourage employees to remain on-site.

☐   Reduce the research and production development cycle time.

☐   Enhance recruiting.

☐   Provide support services in the most cost-effective manner.

☐   Create a competitive advantage.

☐   Extend the endurance and creativity of people.

6.4   Operational Considerations of Communication

Appropriate support services in facilities can improve communication patterns. There is also evidence that the level of communication impacts on organizational performance.

☐   Typically, 60% of the technical information for a project is communicated through informal meetings.

☐   Performance is proportional to the level of interaction among colleagues within the organization.

☐   Interaction with colleagues outside of the immediate project team is conducive to higher performance.

☐   The distance separating workers is the most important factor in determining the likelihood of communication among them.

☐ In general, most daily communication among workers occurs within a distance of 30 meters of their work area.

☐ Group affiliation (by department or project team) also increases the likelihood of communication. Distance has the same effect on a group area as an individual area.

☐ Vertical separation is as much of a deterrent as horizontal separation. People are just as reluctant to use an elevator or climb stairs as they are to walk down a hallway.

6.5   Support and Service Amenities Critical to Communication

☐ Transportation and parking services

- employee
- visitor
- other

☐ Public and visitor services

- employee entrance (dedicated security)
- visitor entrance
- exhibits/displays
- clients demonstration/presentation
- culture center

☐ Meeting and assembly services

- project rooms

- conferencing
- video conferencing
- training
- auditorium/large group assembly
- cafetorium

☐ Technical information services

- library
- document control/records management
- publications
- translation
- self-paced learning rooms
- private rooms

☐ Employee and convenience services

- medical facilities
- fitness center
- showers and locker rooms
- child care
- dormitory
- convenience/company store
- bank/ATM/credit union
- travel agent
- beauty shop / barber shop
- laundry service

☐ Food services

- kitchen and serving
- dining areas
- vending machine areas
- kitchenette facilities
- coffee bars

☐ Circulation and interaction facilities

- atriums and passages
- walkways
- nodes/ lounges
- courtyards

☐ Information and communication system services

- computer center
- data networks
- telecommunications
- power supply
- television and video control center

☐ Office and laboratory services

- audio-visual equipment
- printing and copying
- office supplies
- model shop
- glass shop
- glass washing and storage
- laboratory supplies

☐ Material handling services

- shipping and receiving
- warehousing
- chemicals and hazardous materials
- recycling
- mail and package delivery

☐ Security and safety services

- control center
- security station
- guards

☐ Building and site services

- FM-CADD/CAM
- building control room
- custodial and janitorial
- building/grounds maintenance
- outdoor recreation/jogging trail

Section 7

Cost Effectiveness

Human Factors to Be Considered

Biomechanical :
- ☐ Balance
- ☐ Coordination
- ☐ Sitting
- ☐ Standing
- ☐ Head Movement
- ☐ Lifting/Reaching
- ☐ Handling and Fingering
- ☐ Use of Upper Extremities
- ☐ Use of Lower Extremities
- ☐ Stamina

Sensory:
- ☐ Vision
- ☐ Hearing
- ☐ Olfactory
- ☐ Speech
- ☐ Skin

Psychological:
- ☐ Stress - Fatigue

Intellectual:
- ☐ Coordination
- ☐ Concentration

The importance of cost effectiveness in ergonomics is to evaluate the effectiveness of vended products, hardware, procedures, equipment and personnel within the context of an organizational system. It is important, in other words, to verify that "they do what they say they do." The evaluation of worker interface with tools and equipment determines the effect of these on the higher potentials of human performance. Cost effectiveness can be evaluated by experimental procedures, such as definition of a hypothesis, and manipulation of conditions to evaluate performance and job routines. Test conditions can be developed to simulate as closely as possible what would naturally occur in a real work situation. Of particular interest in ergonomics is the study of worker profiles that represent the population of workers in real situations with attendant stresses and strains. An adequate number of repeated observations or trials must take place in order to give a valid and reliable representation. Cost effectiveness in ergonomics is the evaluation of performance, not price.

7.1   Ergonomic Design Benefits

☐   Improved design

☐   Improved safety

☐   Legal compliance

7.2   Consequences of Not Using Ergonomic Design

☐   Lost time

☐   Increased cost

☐   Legal citation

☐   Injury, illness

☐   Disease

☐   Fatality

☐   Lost quality

7.3   Cost-Related Decisions that Must Be Made

☐   Cost of ergonomics

☐ Choice among equipment purchase options

☐ Decisions about whether to replace or repair equipment

☐ Determination of the value of more efficient ergonomic equipment

☐ Comparison of in-house vs. out-sourced ergonomic services

☐ Comparison with other company investment opportunities

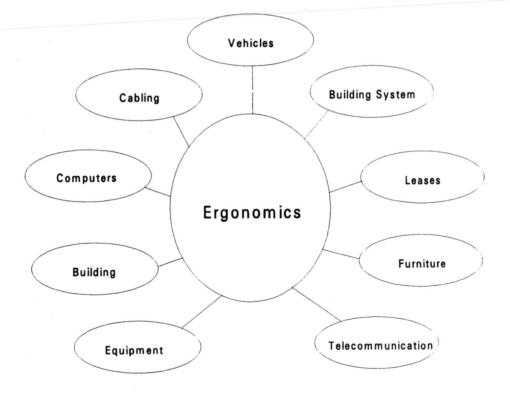

Figure 7-1. Facility Management Asset Resonsibility as Related to Ergonomics.

7.4   Formula of Value

Fortunately, when a basic formula of present value, average annual cost, and internal rate of return is calculated with a computer spreadsheet, the safety manager is able to reach a decision quickly and accurately.

☐   Computer spreadsheets are valuable because they provide the present value, the average annual cost, and the internal rate of return, plus tax depreciation and expected escalation of costs.

7.5   Goal

☐   The goal of cost-effectiveness is to provide the safety manager with a working-knowledge strategy of financial analysis tools combined with a spreadsheet that will convert annual cash flows into numbers suitable for comparison.

7.6   Objectives

☐   An understanding of these terms:

-   present value
-   average annual cost
-   internal rate of return

☐   The ability to calculate and determine when to use each of the above

☐   An understanding of how to use the provided spreadsheet stating the estimated annual costs over the life of the items involved

7.7 Developing an Estimate

Because it relates to ergonomic costs (space planning, furniture, and equipment), developing an elemental estimate is the obvious starting point for developing an estimate. This estimate takes on added significance in ergonomics because it quickly becomes a purchasing document to be used for negotiation of contracts with selected vendors to verify price competitiveness. It is during the actual implementation process that financial management plays its greatest role.

7.7.1 Areas of Financial Management

☐ Establish a project cost accounting system to monitor and control the total ergonomic project cost.

- The system tracks costs associated with various work packages, such as space planning, furniture, electrical equipment, as well as major components within these areas.

☐ Evaluate changes to determine if they are part of the project scope and recommend a course of action, including determining financial responsibility for the changes.

☐ Prepare regular reports summarizing the status of the budget and comparing project progress and schedule.

7.7.2 Information Requirements

☐ To develop an elemental estimate, there are four general pieces of information required:

- organizational mission
- cost limitations
- building size, site, and employee limitations (aging, injury, disease, disability)
- occupancy requirements

☐ With this basic information, the next step is to establish ergonomic design parameters for the proposed building.

The following list shows a typical breakdown of ergonomic classifications for a detailed unit price estimate, and for an elemental estimate.

☐ Ergonomic factors

- accessibility	- lighting
- adaptability	- maintenance (external)
- air quality	- maintenance (internal)
- benchmarking	- material resource conservation
- comfort	- noise
- communication	- passages
- cost-effectiveness	- planning
- density	- relocation
- design	- safety
- division of space	- security
- energy	- signage
- equipment	- software
- finishes	- storage
- furnishings	- temperature
- image	- tools
- instruments	- training

- landscaping	- windows

☐ Unit price estimate

- general requirements	- doors and windows
- site work	- finishes
- concrete	- specialties
- masonry	- equipment
- metals	- furnishings
woods	- special construction
- plastics	- mechanical systems
- thermal protection	- electrical systems
- moisture protection	

☐ Elemental estimate

- foundations	- conveying systems
- subcontractors	- mechanical systems
- superstructures	- electrical systems
- exterior closure	- conditions and profit
- roofing	- equipment
- interior construction	- site work

Elemental estimating enables an ergonomist to stay within the budget by putting the preliminary estimate into the same form as the initial design. During the initial design process, the designer will be forced to make important decisions and trade-offs for each of the various building systems.

☐ Trade-offs

☐ Areas of trade-offs

- legal guidelines (EPA, OSHA)
- price of each system
- appearance and quality
- site complications and restrictions
- owner's special requirements in excess of code requirements
- thermal characteristics
- life cycle costs
- acoustical characteristics
- fire-proofing characteristics

Elemental estimating can help considerably during the stage when these trade-offs are first being considered. If cost is a determining factor, as it often is, then systems estimating can quickly help the designer/ergonomist to determine which option is most cost-effective.

7.8 Cost of Operations as It Relates to Ergonomics

☐ Direct costs to operate the building include ergonomic variable costs and a fixed basic cost.

- maintenance and repairs
- materials and labor
- janitorial cleaning and supplies
- utilities (electric, gas, water, heating oil)
- landscaping, roads, common area
- HVAC
- maintenance worker tools
- vehicles

- service contracts

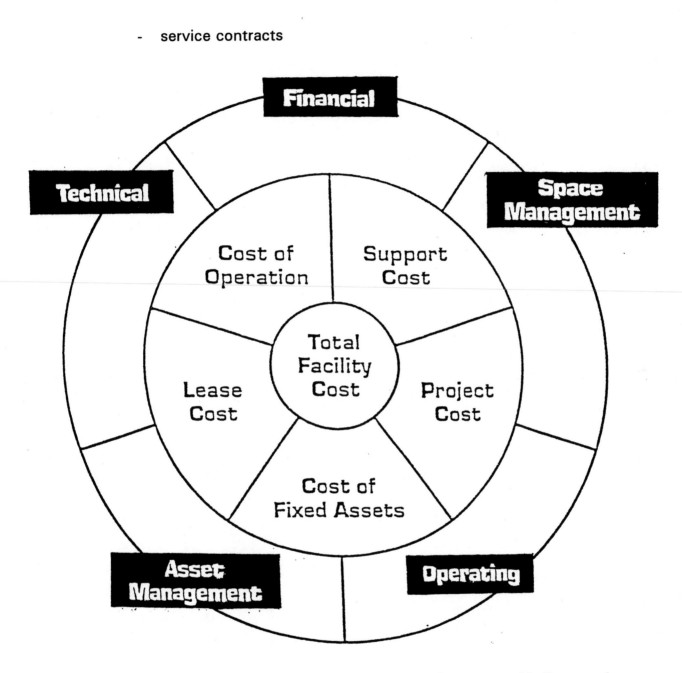

Figure 7-2. Considerations to Measuring Facility Performance with Ergonomic Improvement.

7.8.1 Project Cost

☐ The project cost is the cost required to design, demolish, and renovate workspace that has been previously completed as a capital improvement.

- A/E fees
- demolition cost
- construction
- cabling
- electrical and lighting
- HVAC
- flooring
- relocation

7.9 Factors that Relate Safety Management to Ergonomics

☐ Ergonomics

- vehicles
- building systems
- leases
- furniture
- telecommunication
- equipment
- building
- computers
- cabling

7.9.1 Economic and Client Priority Considerations of Ergonomics

☐   Capital asset management process

- capacity
- security
- appearance
- code violation
- quality
- environment
- asset deterioration rate
- marginal profitability
- cost to defer
- cost to delay
- IRR
- discounted cash flow
- efficiency
- mission support
- effectiveness
- risk reduction
- safety and health

Section 8

Density

```
┌─────────────────────────────────────────────────────────────────────┐
│                    Human Factors to Be Considered                     │
│                                                                       │
│   Biomechanical :                        Sensory:                     │
│       ☐  Balance                             ☐  Vision                │
│       ☐  Coordination                        ☐  Hearing               │
│       ☐  Sitting                             ☐  Olfactory             │
│       ☐  Standing                            ☐  Speech                │
│       ☐  Head Movement                       ☐  Skin                  │
│       ☐  Lifting/Reaching             Psychological:                  │
│       ☐  Handling and Fingering              ☐  Stress - Fatigue      │
│       ☐  Use of Upper Extremities     Intellectual:                   │
│       ☐  Use of Lower Extremities            ☐  Coordination          │
│       ☐  Stamina                             ☐  Concentration         │
│                                                                       │
└─────────────────────────────────────────────────────────────────────┘
```

The ergonomic importance of density is to maintain a balance between employees and their stimulation from the physical environment. Environmental stimulation should not exceed the employee's capacity to scan and process information. Biomechanically, density of equipment, people, materials, or instruments should not impede the direct access to each component. From a sensory perspective, density of stimuli should not overload the senses with excesses of competing noise, glare, smells, or images. Psychologically, density of materials, tools, equipment, or employees should not create a feeling of impingement of the personal space of individuals. Intellectually, density should not interfere with cognitive processes.

8.1 Ergonomic Design Benefits

☐ Improved safety

☐ Legal compliance

8.2 Consequences of Not Using Ergonomic Design

☐ Lost time

☐ Increased cost

☐ Legal citation

☐ Injury, illness

☐ Disease

☐ Fatality

☐ Lost quality

8.3 Design Considerations

☐ Density is a critical focus on the individual workplace and emerging workgroup configurations within organizational settings.

☐ Interior design should clearly demonstrate the advances in interior components and assemblies (ceilings, walls, floors and furnishings), as well as their effective integration with:

- structural systems
- enclosure systems
- mechanical systems
- lighting systems
- telecommunications and power systems

8.3.1 Density Considerations

☐ Air quality

☐ Acoustic quality

☐ Amenities

☐ Connectivity

☐ Shared services

☐ Spatial quality

☐ Thermal quality

☐ Visual quality

☐ Workgroup concepts

☐ Vast open plan

☐ Cluster open plan

☐ Closed offices and shared closed offices

☐ Combi-offices

☐ Free address group address

☐ Caves and commons

☐ Box or universal workstations

☐ Workstations on wheels

☐ Campus and village, indoor-outdoor workplaces

☐ Home, road, and plane offices

8.4 Improvement of Density and Spatial Quality in the Individual Workplace

☐ The question of density is directly related to the size of the workstations and corresponding amenities of work surfaces and storage.

☐ With the redistribution of work responsibilities and related telecommunications equipment, there is a critical need to shift away from the traditional allocation of space size, density, and furniture by rank to allocations by task or function.

- The secretary's workplace must often accommodate computers, typewriters, printers, fax machines, phones, and files.

- A salesperson may be able to effectively function with a phone and a 5 foot work surface, with files, books, and computer networking to complete their task.

☐ Density considerations include the range of tasks and effective workstyles in the determination of workplace size and furniture options.

8.4.1 Improving Workspace Design

☐ Improving the density and spatial quality of workstations is achieved by design. Density considerations include:

- allowing for open systems furniture to evolve into closed offices through stackable panels
- ceiling connections
- three-dimensional space makers

☐ Innovative, high-efficiency storage to relieve the small footprint workstation and to respond to the dual office clutter created by electronics and paper. The paperless office is still years away, and electronics have drastically *increased* the paper produced.

8.4.2 Connectivity in the Individual Workstation

☐ In the electronic workplace, one of the key concerns in density and design is adequate access to data, power, and voice connections.

☐ Several key factors contribute to this effective "connectivity":

- adequate central equipment space
- adequate vertical and horizontal plenum space
- adequate distributed or satellite closets for equipment and networking management
- effective network planning
- effective, modular outlet configurations
- desktop cable management

☐ Density is critical in designing effective workstation and workgroups with the spatial decisions of chairs, work-surfaces, workspace enclosures, and cable management.

☐ There are four interrelated environmental quality agendas and their associated components and subsystems that must be integrated into the four workplace designs:

- visual quality (lighting systems)
- thermal quality (thermal conditioning)
- air quality (ventilation systems)
- acoustic quality (sound generating and canceling systems)

☐ The coordination of acoustic conditioning systems and the spatial defining systems is critical to ensure the necessary visual, thermal, air, and acoustic quality of the workplace.

8.5   Ergonomics and Density

The General Services Administration (GSA) acts as the U.S. government's landlord, managing 254 million square feet of office space. In 1991, GSA issued a new temporary regulation (D-76) on space management. It includes new methods for calculating utilization rates. GSA is now developing new standards for measuring space leased by the federal government from building owners. These standards are also used for measuring space occupied by federal agencies. Hence, GSA is acting as both tenant and landlord. These new standards will include a method for obtaining parity between commercial measurement methods used in different markets and GSA-occupied space.

GSA space measurement is based on logic different from that of BOMA: The actual area available for exclusive tenant use is the governing factor.

8.5.1 Usable Area

☐ Usable area measures the actual occupiable area of a floor or building.

☐ The usable area on a multi-tenant floor can vary over the life of a building as primary corridors change to accommodate tenant access, or as renovations affect building core and service areas.

☐ Usable area is a useful measurement for programming, planning, and allocating space.

8.5.2 Assignable Area

☐ Assignable area excludes secondary circulation space and measures the portion of a floor or building that can actually be used to house personnel, furniture, and equipment. Assignable areas are useful for detailing programming, planning, allocating, and layout of space.

8.5.3 Space Distribution System

☐ Space distribution system specifies the furnishings and finishes necessary for the above work flow, technology, and information systems, such as interior wall systems.

☐ Special items, like a fireplaces or closets, may be important workplace amenities for an executive.

☐ Modular partitioning systems are conducive to maximum productivity and efficiency of space utilization. In the past, these were often incompatible with floor space.

8.5.4 Service Hubs and Shared Equipment

☐ Major innovations in office planning today are the service centers that provide access to:

- copier machines
- laser printers
- new computer equipment
- coffee and breakroom areas

☐ Shared equipment centers are critical to working efficiently today. They can also serve as social centers for the workplace, and should be designed with this in mind.

ABSIC has put forth the concept of a relocatable service hub to serve a working neighborhood of 30-50 people.

☐   This service hub should be an elegant, open social space, central to all the workplaces, and should support a wide range of shared services and attributes.

- coffee, microwave, refrigerator, sink, vending machines
- outputters: color copiers, fax machines, laser printers (with extensive counter adjacent)
- processors: file servers, communication copiers, digitizers, scanners

☐   Characteristics of the service hub:

- dedicated air conditioning and exhaust systems
- critical acoustic absorption (floors, ceilings, behind equipment)
- generous storage area and supplies
- high counters for stand-up discussions
- adjacent seating and views for sit-down discussions
- direct access to the outside

8.5.5 Conference Hubs

It is time for the conference room to come into the electronic age. Presently, most conference rooms up to 600 square feet have abysmal technical resolution with slide projectors and screens and overheads and phones cluttering corners and conference tables, uncontrollable noise and heat releases, and unsafe power connections. Add to this the requirements of computer and video presentation, and teleconferencing and most conference rooms are seriously out-of-date.

The present conference room looks and performs like an electronic storage room.

☐   Develop a consolidated conference hub, one that is visually and physically compact, which enables the room to effectively use the slides, transparencies, and videos that are standard today.

☐   This compact center should be capable of accommodating employees and such audiovisual equipment as:

- wide screen TV, VCR, projection TV, 2 video cameras
- PC projector, PC, scribe position PC, controllers
- dual slide projection, high resolution overhead projection
- electronic whiteboards, information display boards
- fax, telephone, speakers (two way audio)
- data and power links
- sight line optimization
- dedicated air conditioning, exhaust systems
- critical acoustic absorption
- remote infrared controllers or laptops with radio bases
- one dozen notebooks, radio linked with split screen displays for "conferencing"

For tomorrow, ABSIC envisions a conference facility where all inputs will become digital for projection within and transmission to a network of conference centers. In the university setting, this capacity would enable an outstanding faculty member to teach a class simultaneously at many universities, allowing students to receive the best and broadest in course offerings through multi-campus teleconferencing.

Section 9

Design

```
┌─────────────────────────────────────────────────────────────┐
│              Human Factors to Be Considered                   │
│                                                               │
│  Biomechanical :                    Sensory:                  │
│      ☐  Balance                        ☐  Vision              │
│      ☐  Coordination                   ☐  Hearing            │
│      ☐  Sitting                        ☐  Olfactory          │
│      ☐  Standing                       ☐  Speech             │
│      ☐  Head Movement                  ☐  Skin               │
│      ☐  Lifting/Reaching           Psychological:            │
│      ☐  Handling and Fingering         ☐  Stress - Fatigue   │
│      ☐  Use of Upper Extremities   Intellectual:             │
│      ☐  Use of Lower Extremities       ☐  Coordination       │
│      ☐  Stamina                        ☐  Concentration      │
└─────────────────────────────────────────────────────────────┘
```

Design is critical to ergonomics as a systematic planned approach to using all the relevant characteristics of employees (biomechanics, senses, psychology, intellect) to create the optimum interface between these employees and man-made objects, operational facilities, and working environments. Ergonomic design should enhance productivity and efficiency by reducing stresses and fatigues so that employees can work productively, safely, and produce high quality work. In ergonomics, design should strive to understand and maintain the unique functional capacities of people in the workplace environment.

☐   Design should consider people with respect to methods of work, materials used, machines, equipment, tools, and instruments as guides.

☐ Design should consider people as using their bodies biomechanically, sensorially, psychologically, and intellectually.

9.1 Ergonomic Design Benefits

☐ Improved safety

☐ Increased productivity

9.2 Consequences of Not Using Ergonomic Design

☐ Lost time

☐ Increased cost

☐ Legal citation

☐ Lost quality

9.3 Ergonomic Design and Amenity Services

Support and amenities in facilities are generally shared by all workers. They tend not to be assigned to a specific end-user organization or department. Instead, they are centrally managed for the benefit of all occupants. Each case involves a consistent set of service functions, which are grouped into twelve categories. These categories are the basis of planning guides.

9.3.1 Employee Services

☐ Transportation and parking

☐   Public and visitor services

☐   Meeting and assembly services

☐   Technical information services

☐   Employee and convenience services

☐   Food services

☐   Circulation and interaction facilities

9.3.2 Facility Operations

☐   Information and communication systems

☐   Office and lab support services

☐   Material handling services

☐   Security and safety services

☐   Building and site services

9.3.3 Factors to Be Evaluated

☐   The following factors must be evaluated within the guidelines defined by the American National Standard Organization (ANSI/ASQC Q91-1987, Q92-1987, Q93-1987). The ANSI standards are technology-equivalent to International Standards ISO

9001, 9002, and 9003. World Class Manufacturing, American National Standards for work stations (100/1988) and laws and guidelines from the Occupational Safety and Health Act should also be incorporated.

- job task
- expected productivity rates
- stressors
- elimination of employee musculoskeletal stressors
- measurement of working area
- review of employees' use of shared equipment
- assessment of:
  - accessible lighting
  - adaptability maintenance (external)
  - air quality maintenance (internal)
  - benchmarking noise
  - comfort of passages
  - communication planning
  - cost-effectiveness relocation
  - density resource conservation
  - design safety
  - division of space, security, energy, and signange
  - equipment software
  - finishes storage
  - furnishings temperature
  - image tools
  - instruments training
  - windows landscaping
- design of the employees' work stations, support equipment and radius of work areas

- evaluation of seating
- evaluation of support equipment
- review of total physical plant as each worker interacts with the work environment

☐ Design of work areas, surfaces, and tools where technologies must be integrated into other key design factors that satisfy the expectations of both the SUPERVISOR and EMPLOYEE.

9.3.4 What Employers Want to Know

Employers want to know if the work site design makes the best use of:

☐ Esthetics and image

☐ Ease of maintenance

☐ Function and fitness

☐ Lowered first costs and life cycle costs

☐ Responsiveness of a status-marking system

☐ Bulk purchase agreements or existing inventory

9.4.5 Satisfying Criteria while Meeting Corporate Standards, Laws, and Guidelines

Employers want to know if the rooms satisfies criteria while meeting corporate standards, laws, and guidelines of:

- ☐ Appearance

- ☐ Comfort

- ☐ Ease of communication

- ☐ Ease of participation

- ☐ Flexibility

- ☐ Layout

- ☐ Occupancy level

- ☐ Relocation frequency

- ☐ Safety (rules posted)

  - equipment grounded
  - no extension cords
  - safe smoking areas
  - rugs secure

9.3.6 What Both Employees and Employers Want to Know

Both employees and employers want to know if the room provides the appropriate atmosphere by:

- ☐ Increasing opportunities for individual choice

☐ Encouraging independence

☐ Compensating for changes in perception and sensory acuity

☐ Decreasing unnecessary mobility

☐ Encouraging social interaction

☐ Stimulating participation in activities offered

☐ Reducing conflict and distraction

☐ Providing a safe environment

☐ Making activities accessible

☐ Improving employer and employee image

☐ Allowing for growth and change in individuals

9.3.7 Design Recommendations

☐ Taking into consideration the environmental design and specific individual design factors and work environments, work stations and work technologies should be uniquely designed for individual capabilities.

☐ These recommendations illustrate the range of customized options that increase productivity while reducing stress and fatigue.

9.3.8 Quality Check Considerations

☐ Are tasks performed more efficiently?

☐ Are productivity rates maintained or exceeded?

☐ Are stressors diminished?

☐ Have muscular stressors been eliminated?

☐ Have injuries and symptoms been reduced?

☐ Is the physical relationship with equipment well integrated for the employee?

☐ Are accessories within easy reach?

☐ Are there resources for performing the tasks?

☐ Has the intensity of concentration required been reduced?

☐ Is the environment totally accessible?

☐ Have the individual's limitations been mitigated by well-integrated interventions?

☐ What effect have the interventions had on other employees and supervisors?

Section 10

Division of Space

```
┌─────────────────────────────────────────────────────────────────┐
│                  Human Factors to Be Considered                   │
│                                                                   │
│  Biomechanical :                    Sensory:                      │
│      ☐  Balance                         ☐  Vision                 │
│      ☐  Coordination                    ☐  Hearing                │
│      ☐  Sitting                         ☐  Olfactory              │
│      ☐  Standing                        ☐  Speech                 │
│      ☐  Head Movement                   ☐  Skin                   │
│      ☐  Lifting/Reaching            Psychological:                │
│      ☐  Handling and Fingering          ☐  Stress - Fatigue       │
│      ☐  Use of Upper Extremities    Intellectual:                 │
│      ☐  Use of Lower Extremities        ☐  Coordination           │
│      ☐  Stamina                         ☐  Concentration          │
│                                                                   │
└─────────────────────────────────────────────────────────────────┘
```

The ergonomic importance of the division of space is to provide for the broad-based fulfillment of criteria that are necessary for work performance. Division of space biomechanically provides an opportunity for both interaction and privacy within a primary work area. Secondary division of space issues to consider are mobility, convenience, safety, and security of employees when accessing areas for resources, food, or personal hygiene. Psychologically, the division of space is relevant to an emloyee's feeling of aesthetics, values, and security. Intellectually, division of space should account for a necessary size in which tasks can be accomplished without an undo burden of resource support (heat, water) and in proximity to all necessary resources. Division of space should create a natural flow for employees from private workspace to shared areas.

10.1 Ergonomic Design Benefits

☐ Improved safety

☐ Legal compliance

10.2 Consequences of Not Using Ergonomic Design

☐ Lost time

☐ Increased cost

☐ Legal citation

☐ Lost quality

10.3 Workplace Use

☐ Workplaces are used to accomplish work and social leisure activities. This includes multiple settings within the "organizational complex" of facilities as well as remote suburban locations and at-home work.

10.3.1 Working at Many Locations

☐ The goal of planning ergonomics is to acknowledge that employees can work at many locations within a set of facilities (e.g., plant, laboratory, corporate offices) as well as "off-site" and at-home offices.

☐ Providing workplaces at a variety of these locations is part of safety management. The workplaces are not always traditional.

☐ Nontraditional workplaces include:

- enclosed workrooms shared by many people at different times
- quiet lounges with personnel charts or caddies for storage and laptop computers
- suites of offices in suburban shopping centers used as satellite locations

☐ Home offices are being utilized by 20% of working professionals.

☐ The at-home worker can be employed at any professional level within the organization. These workers are not necessarily a remote workforce, nor are they full-time, at-home workers.

☐ The amount of at-home work is individually negotiated. Employees can stay networked and integrated into ongoing business

☐ All management and safety prerogatives should be maintained at all work locations.

10.3.2 Changing Office Approaches

☐ Companies using adaptability of worksites can often attract "non-traditional" workers. The idea behind all these "officing alternatives" is not necessarily to save space or reduce usable square feet per person; this is often a by-product.

☐ Ergonomics helps to match the workplace to the way people and the corporation to maintain productivity and efficiency.

10.4 Ergonomics of the Shared Office

The world's business environment is changing, as are individual workers and the workplace. The operational issues in these future places of work are many. The following are a few examples that apply to different "officing approaches."

☐ The goal of ergonomic adaptability is to provide more space and facility per person, while getting more "round the clock shifts in peak times utility" from each space.

☐ The goal is to reduce the amount of space that is unoccupied for significant periods of time, analyzing both the amount of space used and frequency of use to determine space needs.

☐ Design spaces with more immediate adjustability by the individual (desk height, seat, etc.) and more choice locations (e.g. conference room/office, lounge area/mobile office).

☐ Telephone systems, room reservation and location systems are critical to successful shared and just-in-time officing formats.

☐ Shared space is used by employees who spend time out of the office (e.g. sales people, field engineers, auditors, consultants, project managers).

☐ Ergonomically designed shared offices result in space savings and annual cost savings. Salaries for housekeeping and maintenance have subtracted from the cost savings when aggregated to include all appropriate maintenance savings for a company of 1,000 employees could be 1 million dollars in leased space.

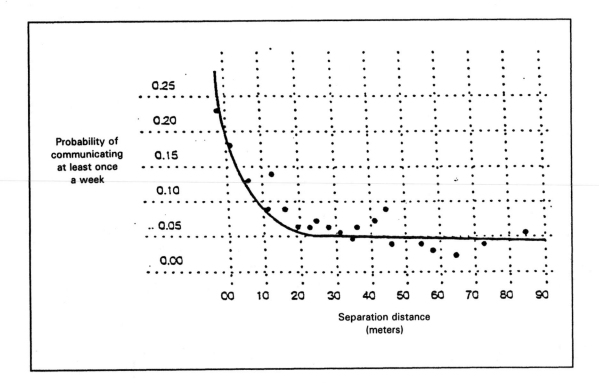

Figure 10-1. Impact of Distance Separating Workers.

10.4.1 Non-Territorial Spaces

☐ A group of employees share a single work area with no defined personal workspace.

☐ All employees share files, library or resource areas, lab space, large worktables, and quiet spaces.

☐ Ergonomic adaptability encourages group and team interaction, and the "fortuitous encounter."

☐ Ergonomics encourages increased employee interaction, which shortens development cycles and improves productivity and work quality.

☐ Non-territorial spaces can be used for development engineers, temporary task forces, multidisciplinary teams, and temporary workers.

10.4.2 Free Address

☐ Free address is a term used primarily in Japan. The goal, depending on the type of employee facilitated, is the same as the non-territorial space, shared spaces and just in-time office.

10.4.3 Home Base/Cave and Commons

☐ Each employee has a small, dedicated office and employees share a variety of open, group spaces (large worktables, lounge areas, terminals, media space, etc.) with the work team.

☐ The goal is similar to the non-territorial space, with the exception that individuals have a private space of their own.

10.4.4 Telecommuting

☐ Employees work at home, in the field at a client site, at a remote corporate facility, as well as in the headquarters' offices.

☐ Telecommuting allows people the flexibility of working at home or at a remote office while also having some base of operation at corporate facilities.

☐ Typically the telecommunter's workspace is small or shared. The goal is to put workplaces at the most convenient location to the worker and his or her work.

☐ The company may supply equipment and furnishings for the home or remote office setting.

10.4.5 Media Space

☐ Media spaces are individual and/or team spaces that have both video and audio recording and receiving capabilities. The theory is that "you don't have to be there to be there."

☐ The goal of using media space is to overcome both time and space limitations.

- Primarily used by development engineers and designers to keep in constant contact with remote design and engineering collaborators and production facilities.
- Will ultimately expand to many other types of workers.

☐ The media space is a success when a larger number of team members have access to more information, more often. Projects are completed faster with fewer errors.

10.4.6 Operational Issues on Non-Traditional Spaces

The idea of all these "officing alternatives" is not necessarily to save space or reduce usable square feet per person. This is often a by-product. Matching the individual to method of work in places acknowledges that corporations are made up of people working. The world business environment is changing, as are individual workers and their workplaces. The operational issues in these future places of work are many.

10.5 Ergonomic Adaptability at Work

☐ Goals and measurements require clear goal setting to:

- save space
- increase access to more space
- enhance individual flexibility of work hours and location
- increase group interaction
- decrease office reconstruction time
- increase user satisfaction
- increase individual or group productivity
- increase space utilization, etc.

☐ Requires both quantitative and qualitative measurement of results.

☐ Requires increased participation by users to work out administrative details of:

- shared equipment
- files
- space

- overlapping work hours
- secretarial support
- check-in/check-out process
- additional support services
- actual job design

☐ Facility requirements:

- increasingly adjustable furniture and equipment by the individual
- increased meeting and group workroom space
- opportunities for selective and absolute privacy
- different dispersal, mix, and design of individually occupied space
- space to be analyzed and distributed in terms of "times and frequency of use" as well as "amount of space needed per person"

☐ Technology requirements:

- increased use of equipment (e.g., mobile phones, terminals, videos, recorders)
- increased variety of worksurface, wires, and amount of space needed for equipment
- increase in the number of and flexibility in operations and distribution of data lines and connectors, telephones, faxes, printers, mobile phones, etc.

☐ Operations requirements:

- increased housekeeping staff for shared or JIT space

- individual and group job design
- administrative office procedures that include check-in and out, location aids, etc.
- inventory of equipment and furnishings in more locations, in often smaller numbers
- managing space at often multiple, small, leased sites

☐ The changing workplace is being used as a tool for management to:

- accommodate individual choice
- reward individual initiative
- accommodate both the amount of space needed and the time space is needed
- support increasingly collaborative work
- adapt to a mobile workforce and workplace
- be a resource that must be more fiscally responsive

10.5.1 Changing Work Styles

☐ The use of traditional work settings—one person, one space, eight hours a day, in centralized corporate spaces—will undoubtedly change over the next ten to fifteen years.

☐ Not all employees will be working in redefined places of work. However, even if 10% of Xerox's employees at roughly 100 sites needed a "non-traditional" work setting, 11,400 employees would be affected.

☐ Technology is dramatically changing work styles. These changes allow the shift from city central and suburban life styles to sub-suburban and remote settings.

☐ Labor shortages could actually increase productivity by forcing corporations to deploy future and existing labor in more creative ways.

- Increased numbers of women, aging workers, and more educated workers are changing the work force profile, and with it, worker demands.

- The need to interact "personally" with more people, more frequently, both in the immediate neighborhood and the world community, over a 24-hour world workday makes change a necessity.

10.6 Adaptability and Productivity

Those of us who perform safety engineering work for corporations and their employees must be aware of how work is changing and of the implications of how we ergonomically forecast, design, manage, and deliver work settings for the future.

Productivity, at an ever-increasing rate, and adaptability, at an ever-expanding definition, are watchwords for the corporation, and ergonomic goals for safety management.

Section 11

Energy

```
┌─────────────────────────────────────────────────────────────┐
│                  Human Factors to Be Considered              │
│                                                              │
│  Biomechanical :                    Sensory:                 │
│      ☐  Balance                         ☐  Vision            │
│      ☐  Coordination                    ☐  Hearing           │
│      ☐  Sitting                         ☐  Olfactory         │
│      ☐  Standing                        ☐  Speech            │
│      ☐  Head Movement                   ☐  Skin              │
│      ☐  Lifting/Reaching            Psychological:           │
│      ☐  Handling and Fingering          ☐  Stress - Fatigue  │
│      ☐  Use of Upper Extremities    Intellectual:            │
│      ☐  Use of Lower Extremities        ☐  Coordination      │
│      ☐  Stamina                         ☐  Concentration     │
│                                                              │
└─────────────────────────────────────────────────────────────┘
```

The ergonomic importance of energy is to consider the interface between human actions and work environments in which the objective is to obtain the optimum level of productive activity. The inappropriate use of energy occurs when human energy consumed is wasted, or when the use of energy leads to fatigue and exhaustion, causing occupational illness or injury. The use of human energy at the optimum level is ergonomically acceptable only when the intensity of the effort occurs without stress or strain. Biomechanically, energy should be expended that does not overload the body to the point of damage to the muscles, tendons, or ligaments. Static and dynamic load to the muscles, tendons, and ligaments should be considered, particularly in combinations of force, awkward postures, repetition, and duration. Physiologically, energy should only be expended to the point that the body experiences a small increase in respiratory rate, temperature, blood pressure, heart rate, sinus arrhythmia, and pulse volume. Equally important is the avoidance of pulse deficit and extremely low temperatures. The body should not be stressed or strained by extreme sensory stimulation created by noise, heat, cold, vibration, or brightness. Psychologically, energy should be expended to maintain vigilance to the intellectual requirements of job tasks. Therefore, extremes of boredom and intellectual overload should be considered. For example, watching video screens for long periods of time with no interaction (e.g., security guards) is extremely boring. That, in contrast to watching video screens that require constant vigilance and tweaking to avoid machine failure is too intense (e.g., job start-ups on new equipment). Human energy should be conserved in the same manner as resourced energy (electricity, water, and fuel).

11.1 Ergonomic Design Benefits

☐　Improved safety

☐　Improved use of energy

☐　Cost reduction

☐　Legal compliance

11.2 Consequences of Not Using Ergonomic Design

☐　Increased cost

11.3 Energy/Resource Management

☐ Telecommunications planning plays a significant part in managing the nation's energy and resources.

☐ Misuse of telecommunications hardware contributes to a wide range of problems in the modern office and results in unnecessary energy usage, including:

- excessive plug loads, even when idle
- excessive ambient light levels
- ineffective task lighting
- inadequate daylight utilization
- overheating and a demand for additional cooling
- unmanageable air distribution patterns
- excessive peak loads
- inadequate sub-metering
- the serious problem of equipment disposal, as it is rapidly exchanged for something newer and better

11.4 Legislative Milestones

☐ In 1975, the Energy Policy and Conservation Act (EPCA) was enacted and addressed energy conservation issues in the Federal government. It included energy management goals for the operation and procurement of buildings, and also required that the Federal automotive fleet meet or exceed the corporate average fuel economy (CAFE) standards.

☐ In 1977, Executive Order (EO) 12003, issued by the President, established a goal to reduce energy consumption in Federal buildings by twenty percent (on a per square foot basis) by the year 1985, as compared to 1975. This EO also established life-cycle standards for government decision-makers.

☐ In 1978, the National Energy Conservation Policy Act (NECPA) further extended the management goals first promoted by EPCA and EO 12003.

☐ In 1982, Executive Order 12375 amended EO 11912 and EO 12003 and relaxed the requirements for the Federal fleet to meet the CAFE standards.

☐ In 1988, the Federal Energy Management Improvement Act (FEMIA) established a goal to reduce energy consumption in Federal buildings by ten percent by 1995, as compared to 1985.

☐ In 1991, Executive Order 1259 further mandated energy consumption reduction goals for buildings and industrial facilities by twenty percent by the year 2000, as compared to 1985.

11.4.1 Past Accomplishments

☐ Between 1973 and 1975, GSA reduced energy consumption by approximately 25% by implementing low cost/no cost operations and maintenance improvement.

☐ Between 1975 and 1985, GSA further reduced its energy consumption by more than 20% by continuing the management practices started in 1973, and implementing energy conservation improvements to its buildings.

☐ Petroleum conservation programs resulted in reducing GSA petroleum use by 75% between 1973 and 1985.

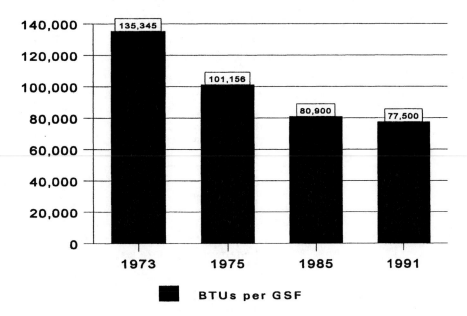

Figure 11-1. GSA's Energy Consumpion Reduction.

☐ New goals established in PL 100-615 and EO 12759, set the course for Federal agencies through the end of this century. The responsibility for implementing these goals falls under each individual agency, with the understanding that each knows the intricacies of its mission and can best incorporate this knowledge into its energy conservation plan.

11.5 Overutilization

☐ Many American industries utilize twice as much energy to produce the same product as their foreign competitors do. The effort to overcome this imbalance of energy overconsumption is an important step toward long-term economic growth.

Title I – Energy Efficiency	
Subtitle A	Buildings
Subtitle B	Utilities
Subtitle C	Appliances and Equipment; Energy Efficiency Standards
Subtitle D	Industrial
Subtitle E	State and Local Assistance
Subtitle F	Federal Agency Energy Management
Subtitle G	Miscellaneous

Figure 11-2. Energy Efficiency under Title I.

11.6 Subtitle E — State and Local Assistance

Subtitle E assists state energy conservation programs by providing million dollar grants to state revolving funds to be used to finance energy efficiency improvements in state and local government buildings. These grants are to be administered by the Secretary of Energy. To be eligible, states must meet three criteria:

☐ Residential and commercial building codes for the state and the majority of local governmental units must meet or exceed CABO and ASHRAE codes, as appropriate.

☐ The state must have an established financing program, including a revolving fund.

☐ The state must have obtained funds from non-Federal sources such as oil-overcharge funds, utility companies (including rebates), and local appropriations, in an amount three times greater than that provided by the Secretary.

11.7 Subtitle F — Federal Agency Energy Management

Subtitle F mandates wide-range Federal energy program requirements, some of which Federal agencies were already complying with from Executive Order 12759.

☐ The Energy Policy Act legally established the same energy consumption reduction goals that were established in Executive Order 12759.

☐ The Federal Energy Management Improvement Act of 1988 had established a 10% reduction goal between fiscal years 1985 and 1995. President Bush expanded that goal in April of 1992, with Executive Order 12759, to a 20% reduction between fiscal years 1985 and 2000.

☐ This subtitle also established the goal of instituting all energy and water conversation measures with a ten-year payback or less by the year 2005

- This is the first time since the 1970's that water conservation has come to the forefront.
- The ten-year payback portion of the goal is very difficult for Federal energy managers to get a handle on, or to get serious about.
- As the Act was being drafted, GSA representatives commented that it would be confusing to have two different goals.
- They further said that with technologies changing so rapidly in the energy conservation arena, new fast-payback technologies developed late in the goal period would certainly ensure that no agency would be able to meet this goal.
- It would also require expensive and continual energy audits, which the Federal budget clearly would not fund, in order to have some measures of whether or not the goal was met.

☐ Title I — Energy Efficiency

- Subtitle A—Buildings
- Subtitle B—Utilities
- Subtitle C—Appliances and equipment
            —Energy efficiency standards
- Subtitle D—Industrial
- Subtitle E—State and local assistance
- Subtitle F—Federal agency energy management
- Subtitle G—Miscellaneous

Section 12

Equipment/Controls

Human Factors to Be Considered

Biomechanical :
- ☐ Balance
- ☐ Coordination
- ☐ Sitting
- ☐ Standing
- ☐ Head Movement
- ☐ Lifting/Reaching
- ☐ Handling and Fingering
- ☐ Use of Upper Extremities
- ☐ Use of Lower Extremities
- ☐ Stamina

Sensory:
- ☐ Vision
- ☐ Hearing
- ☐ Olfactory
- ☐ Speech
- ☐ Skin

Psychological:
- ☐ Stress - Fatigue

Intellectual:
- ☐ Coordination
- ☐ Concentration

The ergonomic importance of equipment and controls is a critical preemptive factor to preventing occupational illness and injury. Equipment and controls are an extension of the human capability and should be designed to accomplish "tasks" while preventing stress and strain to the worker. Equipment should perform the work more efficiently than the worker unassisted. Controls for equipment should require a clear psychomotor action by a worker. Individual equipment differences should be considered based on the range of equipment users. Typically lacking in the evaluation of equipment/controls ergonomics is an anthropomorphic database on real workers in real work settings using equipment and controls efficiently. Establishing a database is important to purchasing and redesign decisions.

12.1 Ergonomic Design Benefits

☐ Improved safety

☐ Legal compliance

12.2 Consequences of Not Using Ergonomic Design

☐ Lost time

☐ Increased cost

☐ System failures

☐ Injury, illness

☐ Disease

☐ Fatality

☐ Lost quality

12.3 Controls

☐ Controls are devices that transmit control information to some mechanism or system. They activate, set to discrete positions, manage flow, and enter data. Controls relate to functions.

☐ It is important to consider human factor aspects in "controlling" equipment. In some cases, this requires correct and rapid identification of a control to maintain safety, such as the foot pedal to operate an automobile's braking system.

☐ It is important for controls to have the shape, texture, size, location, color, sequence, operational label, and method to be understood, so they can be accurately used with speed.

12.4 Coding Controls

☐ Shape and texture desirable features

- useful where illumination is low or where device may be identified and operated by feel, without use of vision
- can supplement visual identification
- useful in standardizing controls for identification purposes

☐ Shape and texture undesirable features

- limitation in number of controls that can be identified (fewer for texture than for shape
- use of gloves reduces human discrimination

☐ Location desirable features

- useful where illumination is low or where device may be identified and operated by feel, without use of vision
- can supplement visual identification
- useful in standardizing controls for identification purposes

☐ Location undesirable features

- limitation in number of controls that can be identified
- may increase space requirements
- identification may be as certain (may be desirable to combine with other coding scheme)

☐ Color desirable features

- useful for visual identification
- useful for standardizing controls for identification purposes
- moderate number of coding categories possible

☐ Color undesirable features

- must be viewed directly (but can be combined with some other coding method, such as shape)
- cannot be used under poor illumination
- requires people who have adequate color vision

☐ Labels desirable features

- large number can be identified
- does not require much learning

☐ Labels undesirable features
- must be viewed directly
- cannot be used under poor illumination
- may take additional space

☐ Operational method desirable features

- usually cannot be used incorrectly (control usually is operable in only one way)
- can capitalize on compatible relationships (but not necessarily)

☐ Operational method undesirable features

- must be tried before knowing if correct control has been selected
- specific design might have to incorporate incompatible relationships

12.5 Visual Displays on Equipment Criteria

12.5.1 Quantitative Scales

☐ Digital or open-window is preferable if values remain long enough to read.

☐ Fixed-scale, moving-pointer designs are usually preferable to moving-scale, fixed-pointer designs.

☐ For long scales, moving scale with tape on spools behind panel or a counter plus circular scale has practical advantage over fixed scale.

☐ For values subject to continuous change, display all (or most) of range used (as with circular or horizontal scale).

☐ If two or more items of related information are to be presented, consider integrated display.

☐   Smallest scale unit to be read should be represented on scale by about 0.05 inches or more.

☐   Preferably use marker for each scale unit, unless scale has to be very small.

☐   Use conventional progression system of 1, 2, 3, 4, etc., unless there is reason to do otherwise, with major markers at 0, 10, 20, etc.

☐   Preferable use is a fixed scale with moving pointer (to show trends).

☐   For groups, use circular scales, and arrange null positions systematically for ease of visual scanning, as at 9 o'clock or 12 o'clock position.

☐   Preferably use extended pointers and extended lines between scales

12.5.2 Status Indicators

☐   If basic data represent discrete, independent categories, or if basically quantitative data are always used in terms of such categories, use display that represents each

12.5.3 Signals and Warning Lights

☐   Minimum size used must be consistent with luminance and exposure time.

☐   Red light is more visible with low signal-to-background contrast.

☐ Flash rate for flashing lights of 1 to 10 per second presumably can be detected by most employees.

12.5.4 Representational Displays

☐ Moving element (such as an aircraft) should be depicted against a fixed background (as the horizon).

☐ Graphic displays that depict trends are read better if they are formed with lines rather than with bars.

☐ Pursuit displays usually are easier for people to use than compensatory displays.

☐ Cathode-ray-tube (CRT) displays are most effective when they are seven to nine or more scan lines per mm.

☐ In the design of displays of complex configurations (such as traffic routes and wiring diagrams), avoid unnecessary detail and use schematic representation if consistent with uses

12.5.5 Alphanumeric Displays

☐ Typography of alphanumeric characters (design, size, contrast, etc.) is especially critical under adverse viewing conditions.

☐ Alphanumeric characters should be presented in groups of three or four for optimum short-term memory.

☐ Capital letters and numerals used in visual displays are read most accurately when:

- the ratio of stroke width to height is about 1:6 to 1:8 for black on white and somewhat higher (up to 1:10) for white on black, and
- the width is at least two-thirds the height
- single numbers, 10; single letters, 26; combination

12.5.6 Symbolic Displays

☐ Symbolic displays are designed on the basis of the following perceptual principles:

- figure/ground
- figure boundaries
- closure
- simplicity
- unity

12.6 Technology Systems

How is each employee's activity interconnected with the work of other productive people in a technology system?

☐ Many of today's organizations have enormous numbers of machines and personal computers, fax machines, high-speed copiers, laser printers, archives, and so on.

- These tools, when assembled as a system, directly support the workflow process.
- Overlaying the technology system onto the workflow system will reveal the degree to which the two work together.

☐ There are many innovations for enhancing environmental control at the workstation, with distributed sensors, hand-held or computer screen controllers, integrated diagnostic units (to evaluate power overloading, temperature, light, flow of air) and for resolving acoustic problems (pagers, mouthpieces, silent rings).

☐ The surge in interest in healthier workplaces will result in less noise, heat, and pollution and lower power. The desktop hardware in the office of the future will follow in most if not all of these directions, and will be the fastest changing systems in the workplace.

☐ While area peripherals have a useful life of 3 to 5 years, the building's HVAC and networking structures will have a life of 5 to 10 years, and the structure and enclosure will have a life of about 50 years. It is for this reason that serious investments must be made to make the building "forgiving" or "loose-fit" for the accommodation of rapidly changing peripheral and servicing systems, rather than "tight-fit" to meet only present-day equipment hardware, networking and environmental needs.

Section 13

Finishes

Human Factors to Be Considered

Biomechanical :
- ☐ Balance
- ☐ Coordination
- ☐ Sitting
- ☐ Standing
- ☐ Head Movement
- ☐ Lifting/Reaching
- ☐ Handling and Fingering
- ☐ Use of Upper Extremities
- ☐ Use of Lower Extremities
- ☐ Stamina

Sensory:
- ☐ Vision
- ☐ Hearing
- ☐ Olfactory
- ☐ Speech
- ☐ Skin

Psychological:
- ☐ Stress - Fatigue

Intellectual:
- ☐ Coordination
- ☐ Concentration

The ergonomic importance of finishes is threefold: their aesthetic value, their durability and maintenance, and their safety. Finishes on surfaces should support health and safety for individuals of all functional capacities. For example, workers with bifocals may misperceive stair riser heights unless they are outlined in yellow. Color can be either very psychologically satisfying or disturbing, as well as cognitively confusing. If the workplace environment is multi-cultural, then the communication of color becomes important. For example, white is a symbol of purity and peace to Americans but may not be thought of as such in other cultures.

13.1 Ergonomic Design Benefits

☐ Improved safety

☐ Legal compliance

13.2 Consequences of Not Using Ergonomic Design

☐ Lost time

☐ Increased cost

☐ System failures

☐ Injury, illness, disease, fatality

☐ Lost quality

13.3 Floor Systems

☐ Only when the area's space distribution and usage is known can designers properly specify flooring structures—whether concrete, metal, or wood.

☐ Besides providing a wearing surface, floor systems also may incorporate wiring for electric power transmission, voice and data communication, and even air delivery in some cases.

☐ In considering the importance of flooring as a system instead of just a structural element, specialties like access flooring become commonplace considerations for today's buildings

13.4 Finishes

☐ People require finishes that support personal image and provide safety, e.g. carpets that do not impede mobility with excessive pile depth.

☐ Avoid patterns that are too busy as they may cause confusion.

☐ Wall surfaces should be smooth to prevent abrasions to people leaning on handrails.

☐ Surface coverings should support the health and safety of individuals, no matter what their functional limitations.

☐ All surfaces should be easily maintainable with smooth wall coverings and/or laminated surfaces.

13.5 Floors

☐ All flooring and flooring materials must meet the National Fire Code, Class I.

☐ Level-loop carpeting should be used in areas where people walk in order to provide a pleasant walking surface and reduce glare and noise.

☐ Direct-glue carpeting should be used to prevent slipping and rolling resistance to wheelchairs.

☐ Where water absorbency is an issue, jute backing is safest.

☐ Floors should be relatively light in color, with 30 to 50 percent reflectance.

13.6 Walls

☐ Brick, concrete, and tile are the most resistant to abuse from contact.

☐ Surfaces should be smooth to prevent abrasions.

☐ Glare should be minimized whenever possible. Reflectance should be 40 to 60 percent.

13.7 Ceilings

☐ Texture, pattern-paint, or fabric-cover to provide visual relief and serve as an aid to orientation.

☐ Reflectance should be 70 to 90 percent.

13.8 Color Choices

☐ Creative and innovative use of color through paint and other decorative materials is an easy way to improve a tired facility's aesthetics and move away from the interiors of traditional institutions.

☐ A typical, updated room may now feature artwork, creative use of paint in contrasting tones, and attractive wall coverings with broad appeal.

☐ Color plays a central role in this move away from "institutional" interiors to a warmer, more comfortable look. Today, it's not enough to "paint everything blue" in an attempt to provide a comfortable, calming effect.

☐ Knowing the basics of color and how to use it as a tool are important steps in creating an environment appropriate to today's work environments.

☐ Research has shown that color can influence human behavior. Cool colors, such as blues and greens, calm and soothe. Warm colors, such as reds and yellows, stimulate the senses.

☐ Although no concrete rules on the use of color exist, following some simple guidelines will optimize the placement of color in your facility.

13.9 Color's Impact

☐ How and where colors are used make a dramatic difference based on the size of space, how the space is used, and available light.

☐ Work areas, such as laboratories and workstations, should use cool colors or those with a high ability to reflect light.

☐ Intensive environments such as these function best when colored with light-reflective hues. These tones improve visibility and reduce shadows, which tend to enhance productivity.

☐ By making the work area easier to see, the use of cool colors also helps to ease tension and provide a comfortable, non-distracting environment. Work areas should employ these colors to promote an uplifting and safe environment.

☐ Areas that serve more social needs—like cafeterias, lounges, and lobbies—should employ warmer, bolder colors that help encourage conversation.

☐ Color selection for break rooms depends largely on the duration for which the rooms are used. Today's trend for comfortable break rooms tends to give less time to boredom. As a result, color choices can lean more toward the neutral or pastel palettes, with brighter accent colors adding visual interest.

☐ In older facilities, rooms should provide a balance of color, a mix of contrasting tones, that keeps the space looking fresh and interesting day-in and day-out.

☐ Bear in mind that mature facilities are usually occupied by older workers. This, coupled with the limited availability of natural and artificial light, will make a significant impact on which colors are selected and how they ultimately will appear to the staff's eyes.

13.10 Positive Values

☐ Color communicates value and image.

   - Out-of-date color schemes may inadvertently project a run-down, neglected appearance, while colors reflecting current lifestyles and fashion communicate a successful, well-maintained facility.

☐ The 1996/1997 color palette is bolder than in years past, combining timeless neutrals with such confident shades as sophisticated violets and optimistic yellows.

☐ In manufacturing facilities, the use of the right combination of colors will emphasize positive design elements while minimizing unattractive ones.

☐ The importance of projecting an up-to-date look bears greater significant in quality managed settings where state-of-the-art, high-tech care and services are expected—even demanded—by customers and staff.

☐ Just as the presence of technological devices builds confidence, a facility that projects an up-to-date image reinforces that confidence.

☐ Keep in mind that "up-to-date" doesn't mean trendy. In fact, most "trendy" or "in" looks date themselves more rapidly in the constantly changing environment than in many other settings.

- Trendy or theme approaches (like a Southwestern or 1950s motif) usually work best for hospitality and restaurant surroundings where the mood is light and festive, and time spent there is limited.

☐ In a manufacturing setting where expectations are more serious, it's best to apply the basics of good design by choosing colors based on a range of complimentary combinations and palettes.

☐ The use of color emphasizes positive design elements and minimizes unattractive ones. Color choice draws attention to or away from interior and exterior features. This is especially true in renovation projects where old or existing structures must be incorporated into the updated space.

☐ Handsome finishes, such as natural marble or rare hardwoods, can be showcased by using understated colors that blend and coordinate. This allows the focal point to remain on the material itself.

☐ The unattractive color of a tile or laminate can be downplayed with the introduction of a distinctly different color scheme. For example, painting columns, beams, and pipes in the same color as an adjacent wall or ceiling will have a camouflaging effect.

☐ Defining space with color draws attention to specific areas and highlight physical details.

- Large facilities have depended on color as a coding mechanism for years, enabling visitors and staff to navigate through even the most complicated floor plans by following color-coded signs, maps, or floor markers.

☐ Safety engineers rely on standardized colors designated by the OSH Act and ANSI to call attention to potential physical hazards.

- orange signifies dangerous equipment
- yellow signifies caution or physical hazards

- green signifies first aid stations

These allow workers to locate hazards and safety devices quickly.

13.11 Practical Approach

- [ ] With today's broad range of colors in paints, fabrics, wall coverings, and furnishings, the variety of possible color combinations is endless.

- [ ] Bear in mind that many materials used in the hospitality industry simply are not designed to hold up to the abuse from equipment particulate and harsh cleaning agents.

- [ ] Stick to top quality materials made specifically for the manufacturing setting. These products will help create surroundings that are attractive and practical.

- [ ] Color plays a key role in striking a balance between function and aesthetics.

- [ ] A well-detailed plan for color selections can save time and valuable resources by providing a strategy for future expansion.

- [ ] A well-thought out "color plan" will liven up tired, institutional-looking facilities and help create a positive atmosphere.

Section 14

Furnishings

```
┌─────────────────────────────────────────────────────────────────┐
│                   Human Factors to Be Considered                  │
│                                                                   │
│  Biomechanical :                    Sensory:                      │
│     ☐  Balance                        ☐  Vision                   │
│     ☐  Coordination                   ☐  Hearing                  │
│     ☐  Sitting                        ☐  Olfactory                │
│     ☐  Standing                       ☐  Speech                   │
│     ☐  Head Movement                  ☐  Skin                     │
│     ☐  Lifting/Reaching             Psychological:                │
│     ☐  Handling and Fingering         ☐  Stress - Fatigue         │
│     ☐  Use of Upper Extremities     Intellectual:                 │
│     ☐  Use of Lower Extremities       ☐  Coordination             │
│     ☐  Stamina                        ☐  Concentration            │
│                                                                   │
└─────────────────────────────────────────────────────────────────┘
```

The ergonomic importance of furnishings is to consider the ergonomic design, comfort, and functionality of workstations and seating positions. The idea is to create work areas that support effective tasks and routines while allowing the body to be supported in postures and positions that enhance the work effort without creating stress, strain, and fatigue. The criteria for selecting furnishings should begin with a database of the real worker population to establish the "norms" and outlayers in the work group. Purchasing decisions should be made on performance in the workplace, not just on cost or long-term vendor relationships. Ergonomics is an overused marketing word in the furniture industry. There is no one chair or work station that "fits all." The design criteria for furnishings should consider the comfort and convenience of the users and observers related to the operating work areas. Furnishing considerations fall into several categories of need, such as visual tasks, primary controls to visual tasks (e.g., keyboard to computer monitor), control display relationships (e.g., phone system, adding machines), arrangement of all necessary elements (e.g., microscope, notebook, samples), and consistency with other layouts in the system.

14.1 Ergonomic Design Benefits

☐ Improved safety

☐ Legal compliance

14.2 Consequences of Not Using Ergonomic Design

☐ Lost time

☐ Increased cost

☐ System failures

☐ Injury, illness

☐ Disease

☐ Fatality

☐ Lost quality

14.3 Evaluating and Selecting Ergonomic Furniture and Equipment

The more interesting activities of the office ergonomics team involve evaluating the different kinds of ergonomic products on the market; however, many problems during facilities implementation can occur if certain issues are not considered. It is important to first evaluate existing facilities standards, inventory processes, accounting methods, and procurement procedures before purchasing any new products. The following questions should be asked:

☐ Are any ergonomic products being used now?

☐ What types of ergonomic products need to be evaluated and specified?

☐ What criteria should be used to evaluate the ergonomic products?

☐ Who will oversee product evaluation and specifications?

☐ Will only one product be specified per item or will more than one manufacturer be used?

☐ Where should a prototype area be set up?

☐ What sources can be used to obtain products for evaluation?

☐ What are the existing facility's standards? What ergonomic products can meet these standards? Can these products be integrated into existing panel and furniture systems?

☐ What improvements can be made to ensure the most impact on facility modification?

☐ What physical properties need to be considered?

☐ What changes need to be made to the facility's standards manual?

14.3.1 Work Station Design

☐ A workstation design that includes seating, work surface, and work-surface technologies is intended to maximize the physical capabilities of the worker and to prevent injuries to the body.

☐ The design should allow optimum mobility and variation in positioning in order to improve the five physical conditions known to affect the capacity to work:

- circulation
- movement
- force exertion
- use of the correct muscles for tasks
- recovery time

Section 15

Image

Human Factors to Be Considered

Biomechanical :
- ☐ Balance
- ☐ Coordination
- ☐ Sitting
- ☐ Standing
- ☐ Head Movement
- ☐ Lifting/Reaching
- ☐ Handling and Fingering
- ☐ Use of Upper Extremities
- ☐ Use of Lower Extremities
- ☐ Stamina

Sensory:
- ☐ Vision
- ☐ Hearing
- ☐ Olfactory
- ☐ Speech
- ☐ Skin

Psychological:
- ☐ Stress - Fatigue

Intellectual:
- ☐ Coordination
- ☐ Concentration

Image is an important ergonomic consideration in enhancing the friendliness of an environment. The coordination of color and finishes invites the use of a work area and reduces psychological stress by giving a sense of flow between the user and the environment. The fewer visable wires, the more organized an area is perceived to be. The more art that is added to the vistas of an area, the less constrained the user feels. The more coordinated the overall image is, the more valued employees feel. The more valued an employee feels, the more productive he or she will be. In these ways, image definitely counts.

15.1 Ergonomic Design Benefits

- ☐ Improved safety

☐ Legal compliance

15.3 Consequences of Not Using Ergonomic Design

☐ Lost time

☐ Increased cost

☐ System failures

☐ Injury, illness

☐ Disease

☐ Fatality

☐ Lost quality

15.3 Image (signage, atriums, quiet rooms, finishes)

☐ A facility is unique in its size, configuration, climate, site topography, and relationship to other elements of the environment.

☐ Each facility offers employees different amenities, levels of service, and worksite supports.

☐ Each property has a unique mix of people in business with different backgrounds, interests, ages, and salaries.

☐ The objective of most managers is to maintain a reasonable return on investment.

☐ The design of a facility and the associated construction costs are significant factors in meeting the objective of image.

☐ Scope is a term commonly used in designing to describe the number of "image" elements required in a specific project. How many executive areas vs. "bull pen" work sites will there be? Requirements for scope vary depending on the corporate commitment to image.

☐ Image requirements establish the minimum number of design elements for a specific project.

☐ Owners or developers may elect the minimum requirements if, in their judgement, increased image will not provide greater satisfaction.

☐ Marketing surveys and other sources of information are usually available to owners or developers to help determine any appropriate increases in the number of image elements.

15.4 Cost

☐ Cost should not always be a factor. For example, multi-use spaces will cost the same as single-use spaces. In many cases, image features benefit all and the decision to include such features is simply a marketing decision.

☐ Each case requires judgement. Therefore, developers and designers are encouraged to examine alternatives, not simply to provide the minimum number of image elements.

Precise analysis of costs for image features cannot be provided in this book because of the wide range of sizes and finishes in standard designs for facilities. Costs also vary for different functional areas within a property and are affected by the total number of elements constructed. Design features generally have a relatively higher cost in smaller and less expensive properties.

15.4.1 Simple Total Cost

A common problem in facility management occurs when purchase decisions are made without consideration for the cost of operation. In the following example, two items are compared that have different initial costs and different annual operating costs.

Section 16

Landscaping

```
┌─────────────────────────────────────────────────────────────┐
│                   Human Factors to Be Considered             │
│                                                               │
│  Biomechanical :                    Sensory:                  │
│      ☐  Balance                        ☐  Vision              │
│      ☐  Coordination                   ☐  Hearing             │
│      ☐  Sitting                        ☐  Olfactory           │
│      ☐  Standing                       ☐  Speech              │
│      ☐  Head Movement                  ☐  Skin                │
│      ☐  Lifting/Reaching            Psychological:            │
│      ☐  Handling and Fingering         ☐  Stress - Fatigue    │
│      ☐  Use of Upper Extremities    Intellectual:             │
│      ☐  Use of Lower Extremities       ☐  Coordination        │
│      ☐  Stamina                        ☐  Concentration       │
│                                                               │
└─────────────────────────────────────────────────────────────┘
```

The ergonomic importance of landscaping is primarily psychological in that it is the official greeter of the workers when they arrive at work. Attractive landscaping can soften a mood and make an employee feel a part of an aesthetically pleasig environment. In this era of windowless environments, landscaping is an essential "escape."

16.1 Ergonomic Design Benefits

☐   Improved safety

☐   Increased image

16.2 Consequences of Not Using Ergonomic Design

☐ Lost time

☐ Injury, illness

☐ Disease

☐ Fatality

16.3 Gardening Considerations

☐ Garden in areas of non-polluted air, sun, wind, with consideration of vegetation for shading, water management, and pesticide safety.

☐ Use proper drainage systems to prevent puddling or flooding.

16.4 Design of Outdoor Spaces

☐ Employee recreation areas should offer protection from the elements.

☐ In hot climates, a portion of the outdoor space should be protected by shade devices such as umbrellas, trellises, or deciduous trees.

☐ Walls or trees can provide protection from strong prevailing winds.

☐ Remote outdoor spaces or recreation areas should include canopies or similar protection from sudden rain showers.

16.5 Accessible Facilities

☐ Raised planters allow wheelchair users to see, touch, and smell flowers and plants. (Accessible restrooms, telephones, drinking fountains, and other public facilities should also be available within a convenient travel distance.)

☐ All walkways should have paved, smooth surfaces.

☐ Ramps or lifts should be provided at vertical level changes.

☐ Where outdoor dining is provided, aisles, tables, and chairs should meet the requirements for accessibility.

16.5.1 Accessible Outdoor Spaces

☐ Terraces, gardens, pool decks, game areas, or other outdoor recreation spaces should be designed for the use and enjoyment of employees with restricted capabilities.

- To help meet this objective, these outdoor spaces should be connected to the building's accessible routes.

16.5.2 Rest Areas

☐ Provide rest areas on long walkways that connect elements such as gardens, docks, golf courses, or tennis courts.

☐ Rest areas should provide protection from adverse elements and to take advantage of site amenities. These areas should include seating, trash receptacles, and lighting, where possible.

☐ Selected rest stops on long walks or trails should include facilities such as drinking fountains, canopies, and restrooms.

16.5.3 Benches

☐ Outdoor benches should have adequately designed backs and armrests.

- The benchseat should be 16" to 18" from front to back and be approximately 18" above the ground.
- The seat should decline slightly to the rear for comfort and to drain rainwater.

☐ Benches and trash receptacles should be located at least one foot from the edges of the paved walking surface.

☐ A three-foot-wide paved, open space is recommended adjacent to benches for wheelchair seating or strollers.

16.5.4 Signage

☐ Clear directional signage is important for orientation.

☐ Signs should be mounted at eye-level, approximately five feet above the walkway.

☐   The signs and surface of the walkway should be illuminated for night use.

Section 17

Lighting

```
┌─────────────────────────────────────────────────────────────────┐
│                  Human Factors to Be Considered                   │
│                                                                   │
│  Biomechanical :                      Sensory:                    │
│      ☐  Balance                          ☐  Vision                │
│      ☐  Coordination                     ☐  Hearing               │
│      ☐  Sitting                          ☐  Olfactory             │
│      ☐  Standing                         ☐  Speech                │
│      ☐  Head Movement                    ☐  Skin                  │
│      ☐  Lifting/Reaching              Psychological:              │
│      ☐  Handling and Fingering           ☐  Stress - Fatigue      │
│      ☐  Use of Upper Extremities      Intellectual:               │
│      ☐  Use of Lower Extremities         ☐  Coordination          │
│      ☐  Stamina                          ☐  Concentration         │
│                                                                   │
└─────────────────────────────────────────────────────────────────┘
```

Lighting strategy is most frequently part of an architectural plan of workplace form and function. Over time, lighting is often on the forefront of the cost reduction attack (e.g., saving money and ozone by cutting lights.) Yet lighting to task is one of the most important factors in ergonomics. Light affects the ability of employees to see, particularly as they age. Light attracts people to space while darkness deters them from it. For example, people will linger in an area that has higher light levels (people talking in passageways) and move more quickly through dark areas (storage). Light also affects the way people feel. Some people need more light to eliminate the depression of seasonal affective disorders. By manipulation of lighting to forms, textures, color renderings, and specifically to the needs of a task, lighting can evoke many different and desired responses from the employee. For example, lighting in stock rooms should allow for the easy reading of labels and identification of stored items. A lighting system should be developed that is a general pattern system and a focal system and that permits switching and dimming controls to specific areas. Lighting should always be an integral part of an ergonomic design to enhance visual acuity.

17.1 Ergonomic Design Benefits

☐   Improved safety

☐   Legal compliance

17.2 Consequences of Not Using Ergonomic Design

☐   Lost time

☐   Injury, illness

☐   Disease

☐   Fatality

☐   Lost quality

☐   Increased cost

☐   Legal citation

17.3 Suggested Lighting

☐   Parabolic louvers to eliminate screen reflection

☐ Dimmers for task-ambient levels

☐ Daylight sensors

☐ Pigtail or tether systems for relocatability

☐ Radio frequency or infrared remote controllers

☐ Uplighting

☐ Covelighting/ceiling configurations

☐ Daylight interface with electric lighting

☐ Wall, floor, and furniture task and ambient fixtures

☐ Two-adjustable-arm, high efficiency task lamps

☐ Toplighting with high-efficiency reflectors and lenses

☐ Sidelighting with light shelves

☐ Sloped ceilings

☐ Diffuse lighting

☐ Prismatic windows

☐ View of content

17.4 Fluorescent Lighting

☐ The utilization of innovative fluorescent lighting in commercial applications includes the integral compact fluorescent and improved four-foot T8 and T10 fluorescent lamps. Illustrations of their successful application by means of case studies are presented in Table 17-2.

Table 17-1. Standards – Flourescent Lamps				
Lamp Type	Nominal Lamp Wattage	Minimal CRI	Minimum Average Lamp Efficacy (LWP)	Effective Lifetime (Months)
4-foot medium by-pin	〉35W 〈35W	69 45	75.0 75.0	36 36
2-foot U-shaped	〉35W 〈35W	69 45	68.0 74.0	36 36
8-foot slimline	〉65W 〈65W	69 45	80.0 80.0	18 18
8-foot high output	〉100W 〈100W	69 45	80.0 80.0	18 18

☐ The majority of standard T-12 diameter fluorescent lamps available today (and those that do cost as much as the best T-8 or T-10 diameter systems) will not meet these standards.

☐ New T-12 lamps that meet these requirements will be developed; however, the price will be high enough that switching to T-8 lamp technology will most often not be cost-effective.

Table 17-2. Standards – Incandescent Reflector Lamps		
Lamp Wattage	Minimum Average Lamp Efficacy (LPW)	Effective Lifetime (Months)
40-50	10.5	36
51-66	11.0	36
67-85	12.5	36
86-115	14.0	36
116-155	14.5	36
156-205	15.0	36

☐ New standards for lamp efficacy will also be required for incandescent reflector lamps effective three years from the date of passage.

17.5 Changes in the Way of Doing Business

Over the past decade, people have experienced a change in the way they do business in a number of ways.

☐ The office environment, which used to be paperwork-oriented, has changed into an electronically dominated space containing computers, cellular telephones, faxes, and other modern equipment. This metamorphosis has permanently changed the nature of office work and, with it, the office environment.

☐ The way our retail stores market their products has changed, going from a mass-merchandising approach to more successful visual merchandising strategies.

☐ In industry, we are moving away from labor-intensive businesses towards those dominated by automated equipment and systems.

☐ All these changes in society and business have affected the way we use and perceive lighting and have resulted in different demands on modern lighting installations.

17.6 Energy Conservation

One of today's primary requirements for lighting is energy conservation. Lighting consumes approximately 25% of the total electricity used in the business world and is a natural target for the energy and environmental conservation measures encouraged by government, utilities, and other special interest groups.

☐ Light sources have become more energy-efficient, more compact, and better designed for quality visual characteristics.

17.6.1 Recent Developments in Lighting

☐ Compact fluorescent lamps to replace inefficient light sources like incandescent lamps without sacrificing color rendering and light output.

☐ New, innovative fluorescent systems consisting of reduced diameter four-foot lamps, high-efficiency light sources, electronic ballasts, and dimming controls that allow for lower energy consumption while delivering higher quality lighting to commercial spaces.

☐ According to the Environmental Protection Agency (EPA), if all businesses utilized high-efficiency lighting techniques, 11% of the electricity used would be saved (totaling $18.6 billion annually at today's cost).

☐ In addition to energy savings, there would be other environmental benefits, such as a 5% reduction in the atmospheric levels of sulfur dioxide (the primary cause of acid rain), and carbon dioxide, which is believed to contribute to global climatic changes via the greenhouse effect.

☐ Further reductions in the consumption of electricity would curtail the building of new power plants (another benefit to an already over-taxed environment).

17.7 Lighting Considerations

☐ Account for the following lighting considerations:

- prismatic glass
- interior light diffusers/reflectors
- frit glazing, Inverted mini blinds
- light pipes, fiber optics
- interfacing with electric lighting configuration and control
- spatial orientation, depth, ceiling configuration, layout
- specifications for viewing cone, view, content, and clarity

☐ Each development in electric lighting requires parallel developments in the management of daylight glare and brightness contrast, demonstrated so far in only a few innovative projects.

17.8 Lighting Environments

☐ Light quantity and quality play a considerable role in determining office worker productivity.

☐ Natural light through windows should be combined with interior lighting.

☐ A flexible combination of indirect and task lighting should utilize the space distribution system, as opposed to simply using the traditional ceiling system.

17.9 Natural Lighting

☐ Use more effective natural/electric light balancing in order to reduce visual strain from long hours in front of computer screens.

☐ Combining low ambient lighting from daylight and electric light sources with task lighting, locally controlled for individual preferences, time of day, and activity.

17.10 Innovations

☐ Lighting system innovations include:

- continuous dimming fixtures

- individually switched (on/off) fixture
- easily relocatable tether or pigtail fixtures
- shielded fixtures in which neither the image of the bulb nor the lens is reflected on the work surface or the computer screen.

Section 18

Maintenance — Internal

```
┌─────────────────────────────────────────────────────────────┐
│                 Human Factors to Be Considered                │
│                                                               │
│  Biomechanical :                    Sensory:                  │
│     ☐ Balance                          ☐ Vision               │
│     ☐ Coordination                     ☐ Hearing              │
│     ☐ Sitting                          ☐ Olfactory            │
│     ☐ Standing                         ☐ Speech               │
│     ☐ Head Movement                    ☐ Skin                 │
│     ☐ Lifting/Reaching              Psychological:            │
│     ☐ Handling and Fingering           ☐ Stress - Fatigue     │
│     ☐ Use of Upper Extremities      Intellectual:             │
│     ☐ Use of Lower Extremities         ☐ Coordination         │
│     ☐ Stamina                          ☐ Concentration        │
│                                                               │
└─────────────────────────────────────────────────────────────┘
```

The ergonomic importance of internal maintenance is to maintain the equipment and the environment in a manner that promotes safety and equipment efficiency. A preventive maintenance program should be developed that fulfills the needs of the organization to prevent injury and repair costs. Workers need to be part of the maintenance team within their areas in order to promote "ownership" of their physical and intellectual capacities. Work orders on failed equipment should have a routing system and an expected timeline for completion. The machines, equipment, tools, and the workplace environment should permit satisfactory levels of worker performance and provide a safe work environment.

18.1 Ergonomic Design Benefits

☐ Improved safety

☐   Legal compliance

18.2   Consequences of Not Using Ergonomic Design

☐   Lost time

☐   Injury, illness

☐   Disease

☐   Fatality

☐   Lost quality

☐   Increased cost

☐   Legal citation

18.3   Maintenance Responsibility

☐   Proper maintenance yields a productivity improvement of 10 to 15 percent for most organizations. Improvements can occur in both cost reduction and quality.

18.4   How to Reduce Maintenance Costs and Improve Quality

☐   Develop illustrated training manuals to guide staff in specific actions (with considerations for cultural diversity).

    -   EXAMPLE:

A. Spray window fully

B. Wait 30 seconds

C. Wipe clean with paper towel

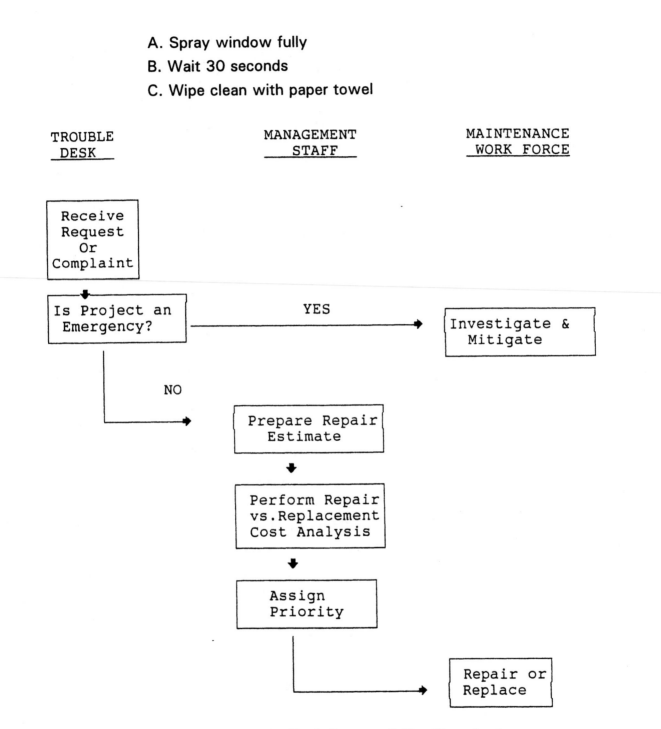

Figure 18-1. Maintenance Task Responsibility Flowchart.

☐ Write clear job descriptions for all workers. Each duty should be outlined.

☐ Use positive titles such as Environmental Service Worker, rather than negative titles such as Janitor.

☐ Train workers properly to ensure the quality of the routines and safety of all employees.

- EXAMPLE:
  Remove carpet stains using stain-removal kits. Each worker assigned to an area containing carpets should be trained and equipped to remove stains. Many times, the successful removal of carpet stains depends solely on how quickly the worker attempts to remove them.

☐ Assign repetitive work (performed more often than monthly) on an area-complete basis.

- This work should be assigned to one person who should perform all routine tasks within the assigned area.
- The work should be measured to ensure a fair assignment and reasonable expectations. This will provide the opportunity to evaluate individual performance and to recognize and reward quality effort.

☐ Supplement the worker performing the routine work with special project teams.

Task	Frequency of Service	
	Computer Rooms	Copy Rooms, Duplicating, Graphics, etc.
Police litter	Daily	Daily
Empty and spot-clean trash receptacles	Daily	Daily
Empty and damp-wipe ash receptacles	Daily	Daily
Replace obviously soiled or torn liners	Daily	Daily
Clean chalk and marker boards	Weekly	Weekly
Provide clean erasers	Daily	Daily
Dust horizontal building and furniture surfaces	Daily	Daily
Dust vertical building and furniture surfaces	Every 2 Weeks	Every 2 Weeks
Polish unsealed wood furniture	As Needed	As Needed
Spot-clean walls, doors, furnishings, and glass	Daily	Daily
Completely clean entrance door glass	Weekly	Weekly
Clean and disinfect water fountains	Daily	Daily
Spot-clean carpet stains	Daily	Daily
Partially vacuum (traffic patterns, obvious soil)	Daily	Daily
Completely vacuum	Weekly	Weekly
Dust-mop or sweep non-carpeted floors	Daily	Daily
Spot-mop non-carpeted floors	Daily	Daily
Damp-mop non-carpeted floors	Every 2 Weeks	Every Weeks
Wet-clean non-carpeted floors	As Needed	As Needed
Spray-buff metal-link finished floors	As Needed	Every 2 Weeks
Refill dispensers	As Needed	As Needed
Disinfect furniture, fixtures, partitions, and walls	As Needed	As Needed
Clean and disinfect sinks, toilets, urinals, and showers	As Needed	As Needed
Damp-mop and disinfect non-carpeted floors	As Needed	As Needed
Descale toilets and urinals	As Needed	As Needed
Clean floor drains	As Needed	As Needed
Replace furniture in proper location	Daily	Daily

Figure 18-2. Sample Routine Work Schedule.

- The project team should perform infrequent labor-intensive tasks, such as stripping and refinishing floors, carpet extraction, window washing, etc.
- The project team should be well trained and utilize special equipment not required by regular workers.

☐ Provide a relief staff to perform the work of absent workers.

- Ensure that each assignment is performed completely as specified should standardize the service to the "customer" and help maintain the desired level of quality.
- Eliminate the practice of regularly pulling workers from their assigned area to perform the work of an absent worker. This will improve the worker's morale.

☐ Eliminate all products containing a "poison" or "flammable" label. There are many products that do not have these characteristics that will do the job.

☐ Avoid standard specialty products such as scouring powder, ammonia, bleach, steel wool, pine oil, etc. As a number of modern cleaning materials cost little more, do not harm the user or the surface on which they are used, and do a much better job.

☐ Let the custodial office be an example for others.

- Maintain a neat and organized desk, remove unprofessional materials and pictures from the walls, and have all equipment and reference material readily available.

- The custodial office should send a message to everyone that the department is well organized and efficient.

Section 19

Material Resource Conservation

Human Factors to Be Considered

Biomechanical :
- ☐ Balance
- ☐ Coordination
- ☐ Sitting
- ☐ Standing
- ☐ Head Movement
- ☐ Lifting/Reaching
- ☐ Handling and Fingering
- ☐ Use of Upper Extremities
- ☐ Use of Lower Extremities
- ☐ Stamina

Sensory:
- ☐ Vision
- ☐ Hearing
- ☐ Olfactory
- ☐ Speech
- ☐ Skin

Psychological:
- ☐ Stress - Fatigue

Intellectual:
- ☐ Coordination
- ☐ Concentration

As we move toward the year 2000, material resource conservation is becoming the responsibility of every organization and every worker. Many organizations are subscribing to the International Standards Organization (ISO) 9000 criteria. Most materials that are conserved for reuse require special handling procedures. Some materials may be set aside for recycling, while others may be "contained as contaminants." In any case, material resource conservation becomes a part of the production process in many facilities and has ergonomic implications because it often involves "material handling" in special ways. Material resource conservation may involve workers in stresses (such as biomechanically lifting or moving) or sensorially (by exposure to minute or large amounts of chemicals.) An ergonomic review of how materials are managed for conservation is often overlooked as a potential for risk reduction.

19.1 Ergonomic Design Benefits

☐ Improved safety

☐ Legal compliance

19.2 Consequences of Not Using Ergonomic Design

☐ Lost time

☐ Injury, illness

☐ Disease

☐ Fatality

☐ Lost quality

19.3 Waste Management and Material Conservation

☐ Establish an aggressive and proactive material conservation management program.

☐ The plan should be flexible enough to meet the challenges and opportunities presented by legislation, regulations, advances in technology, and other influences that will affect the organization's mission.

☐ The next few years will provide unique opportunities for recycling.

- New equipment, technologies, and materials are being developed.
- Future international meetings, legislation, and regulations have been scheduled.
- Laws and regulations are very complex and detailed and will force everyone in business to comply with the new environmental standards.

19.3.1 Objective

☐ The objective is to take appropriate action that will reduce material losses to the lowest practicable or achievable level, and will maximize resource reuse by recovery, recycling, and reclaiming techniques.

19.4 Policy Implementation to Manage Resources

☐ Policy implementation requires:

- development of a general environmental guidance
- awareness of laws and regulations
- understanding of code and standards compliance
- achieving of internal coordination, and keeping up with technological developments

19.4.1 Example: General Guidance in Refrigerants/Safety Risk
Air Quality

Operational units:

☐   Take appropriate action to reduce the loss and risk of ozone-depleting refrigerants.

☐   Improve and expand testing, inspection, and maintenance procedures, equipment enhancements, and refrigerant recovery, recycling, and reclamation.

Units requiring repair:

☐   Conduct lifecycle cost studies to determine whether to repair existing structurally-sound CFC chillers, or to convert these chillers to less environmentally adverse refrigerants, such as HCFCs and HFCs to extend their useful life.

Units needing replacement or new units:

☐   No new CFC chillers should be purchased. HCFC and HFC chillers, absorption machines, and purchased chilled water are acceptable alternatives.

☐   All existing and emerging cost-effective technologies should be considered.

19.5 Terminology

Recycling:

☐   Equipment should draw out refrigerant, remove contaminants, and return cleaned refrigerant.

☐   Refrigerant should be cleaned to meet ARI Standard 700-88.

Recovery:

☐   Equipment should draw refrigerant from a system and store it until reuse.

Reclamation:

☐   Develop a process to restore contaminated refrigerant to ARI Standard 700-88 at a special processing plant.

Section 20

Noise

```
┌─────────────────────────────────────────────────────────────┐
│              Human Factors to Be Considered                  │
│                                                              │
│  Biomechanical :                    Sensory:                 │
│      ☐  Balance                        ☐  Vision             │
│      ☐  Coordination                   ☐  Hearing            │
│      ☐  Sitting                        ☐  Olfactory          │
│      ☐  Standing                       ☐  Speech             │
│      ☐  Head Movement                  ☐  Skin               │
│      ☐  Lifting/Reaching            Psychological:           │
│      ☐  Handling and Fingering         ☐  Stress - Fatigue   │
│      ☐  Use of Upper Extremities    Intellectual:            │
│      ☐  Use of Lower Extremities       ☐  Coordination       │
│      ☐  Stamina                        ☐  Concentration      │
│                                                              │
└─────────────────────────────────────────────────────────────┘
```

The importance of noise to ergonomics is to consider that performance can be adversely affected by noise exposure. It is important to note that people differ in their definition of noise (music, barking dogs, crying children) and in their tolerance for it (decibel levels). In other words, to one listener a softly crying baby can be more stressful than acid rock music at 90 decibels. The lower the person's tolerance for noise, the more noise will affect that person by making him or her feel stressed and fatigued. Noise can negatively affect the performance of mental tasks (e.g., calculations), tasks that require skill and speed (e.g., fine motor repairs), tasks that demand a high level of perceptual capacity (e.g., computer assisted drawing), and tasks that require complex psychomotor skills (e.g., retooling a machine to engineering specifications). An ergonomic strategy of noise reduction should include assessing potentially distracting noise, particularly if the noise is repetitive, ponderous, or unpredictable. Interventions can be developed case-by-case or department-by-department.

20.1 Ergonomic Design Benefits

☐ Improved safety

☐ Legal compliance

20.2 Consequences of Not Using Ergonomic Design

☐ Lost time

☐ Injury, illness

☐ Disease

☐ Fatality

☐ Lost quality

20.3 Suggested Equipment

☐ Office equipment

- hoods for laser and inkjet printers
- low noise processor fans
- adjustable telephone rings
- full mouth pieces

☐   Ceilings, walls, and floors

- acoustic ceilings, partitions, and walls
- levels of enclosure
- acoustic surrounds for printers

☐   Mechanical systems

- acoustically-dampened, no-cycling air systems
- balanced white or pink noise system
- maintained perimeter heating and cooling systems

20.4 Acoustics

Accoustics tend to be among the most ignored priority.

☐   Acoustical problems are typically more of an annoyance than an overwhelming priority.

☐   Many charged with a solution to these problems are not exactly sure how to solve them. The problem often tends to "go away" because people tire of complaining.

☐   While there is very little statistical data about the advantages of good acoustic design, not many would argue with the conclusion that a noisy environment has a negative impact on efficiency in most work situations.

☐ Other spaces, such as auditoriums and cafeterias, have different criteria. In order for architects to be able to identify and resolve acoustic problems, a basic understanding of acoustics is necessary.

20.5 Sound and Its Measurement

☐ Sound is caused by fluctuations in air pressure. These vibrations of the air vibrate our eardrums, and through a network of bones and nerves are transmitted to the brain. The more fluctuations, or cycles per second (Hz), the higher the pitch.

☐ Sound travels through the air at approximately 1120 feet per second (760 mph).

☐ An important quantitative measure of sound is the decibel (dB). This is a unit used to express relative difference in intensity between two acoustic signals, and is equal to ten times the common logarithm of the ratio of the two levels.

20.5.1 The Decibel Scale Is Logarithmic

☐ For practical purposes, each 10 dB increase is perceived as a doubling of the sound level. Conversely, a 10 dB decrease is a reduction by half.

☐ When a decibel level goes from 50 to 40 dB we experience a 50% reduction, not a 20% reduction. In terms of sound energy, a 10 dB increase is ten times greater.

20.5.2 Determination of Noise Reduction

☐   For enclosed areas (complete rooms), use the following procedure:

- Calculate the absorption in the room and the amount of absorption to be added.

| | absorption after treatment (Sa) | | | | | | | | | | |
	absorption before treatment (Sb)										
Above Ratio Equals	1	2	3	4	5	6	7	8	9	10	20
Noise Level (Percentage Change)	0	20	30	35	40	42	45	46	48	50	60
Decibel Change	0	3	4.8	6	7	8	8.5	9	9.5	10	13

Figure 20-1. Acoustic Absorption Rates.

- Acoustic absorption is measured in sabins (Sa) and is calculated by multiplying the square feet of surface area by the NRC of the material on that surface.
  Example: 100 sf xNRC (.85) = 85 Sa.

☐   The absorption change is determined by the ratio found in Figure 20-1.

20.5.3 The OSHA Hearing Conservation Standard

The OSHA Hearing Conservation Standard is printed in 29 CFR 1910.95(c) through (p), and sets forth all applicable OSHA requirements. The standard also has nine appendices (Appendix A through 1). They contain information that is quite helpful. A copy of the OSHA standards on noise exposure and hearing conservation is attached below.

☐   Occupational noise exposure

- (a) Protection against the effects of noise exposure shall be provided when the sound levels exceed those shown in Figure 20.3 when measured on the A scale of a standard sound level meter at slow response.

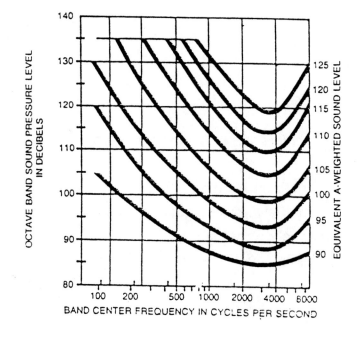

Figure 20-2. Band Center Frequency in Cycles Per Second.

- When noise levels are determined by octave band analysis, the equivalent A-weighted sound level may be determined as shown in Figure 20-2.

20.5.4 Equivalent Sound Level Contours

☐ Octave band sound pressure levels may be converted to the equivalent A-weighted sound level by plotting them on this graph and noting the A-weighted sound level corresponding to the point of highest penetration into the sound level contours. This equivalent A-weighted sound level, which may differ from the actual A-weighted sound level of the noise, is used to determine exposure.

Section 21

Passages

```
┌─────────────────────────────────────────────────────────────┐
│              Human Factors to Be Considered                 │
│                                                             │
│  Biomechanical :                   Sensory:                 │
│    ☐  Balance                        ☐  Vision              │
│    ☐  Coordination                   ☐  Hearing             │
│    ☐  Sitting                        ☐  Olfactory           │
│    ☐  Standing                       ☐  Speech              │
│    ☐  Head Movement                  ☐  Skin                │
│    ☐  Lifting/Reaching             Psychological:           │
│    ☐  Handling and Fingering         ☐  Stress - Fatigue    │
│    ☐  Use of Upper Extremities     Intellectual:            │
│    ☐  Use of Lower Extremities       ☐  Coordination        │
│    ☐  Stamina                        ☐  Concentration       │
│                                                             │
└─────────────────────────────────────────────────────────────┘
```

How workers move through facilities is part of a critical ergonomic evaluation. Slips, trips, and falls are still a major contributor to back and hip injuries. Workers must be allowed safe and clear passage when moving from one part of the facility to another. In addition, all material handling procedures should be reviewed to determine what areas present a high risk.

21.1 Ergonomic Design Benefits

   Improved safety

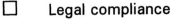   Legal compliance

21.2 Consequences of Not Using Ergonomic Design

☐ Lost time

☐ Injury, illness

☐ Disease

☐ Fatality

☐ Lost quality

21.3 Circulation System

☐ The movement of people between floors can affect productivity.

   - Tom Allen, MIT professor and noted designer of high-tech facilities, suggests that 80 percent of good ideas result from informal communication.

☐ Circulation of workers increases productivity. For that reason, moving stairs and even fixed-stair designs may benefit an organization by getting more people to talk informally away from their work areas, and thus generate more ideas.

21.3.1 Circulation and Interaction Facilities Typical Functions

☐ Facilities that foster interaction serve multiple purposes. In general, they are common or shared-use facilities that are located within a high traffic zone. Not only do they encourage interaction, but they also offer a refuge (or relief) from the primary work area.

☐   The right location, configuration, and operation of these facilities can increase chance encounters and promote informal contacts among occupants. They are sometimes referred to as "magnets" because of their attraction feature. These facilities include:

- restrooms
- copy machines
- coffee stations
- cafeterias
- special equipment areas
- supply rooms
- conference rooms
- other shared areas

☐   Interaction patterns can be further enhanced by facility areas that provide a setting for occupants to stop and meet informally. These facilities include:

- walkways/hallways
- atria
- lobbies
- courtyards
- elevators/escalators/stairwells

21.4 General Considerations

☐ Many factors contribute to making a productive and creative workplace. To be successful, a workplace must help the organization be both efficient and effective.

☐ Increased competition has shortened the effective lifespan of both products and knowledge. An efficient organization must have a shorter elapsed time period from invention to new product introduction than their competitors have.

Planning

```
┌─────────────────────────────────────────────────────────────────┐
│                    Human Factors to Be Considered                 │
│                                                                   │
│  Biomechanical :                      Sensory:                    │
│     ☐  Balance                           ☐  Vision                │
│     ☐  Coordination                      ☐  Hearing               │
│     ☐  Sitting                           ☐  Olfactory             │
│     ☐  Standing                          ☐  Speech                │
│     ☐  Head Movement                     ☐  Skin                  │
│     ☐  Lifting/Reaching               Psychological:              │
│     ☐  Handling and Fingering            ☐  Stress - Fatigue      │
│     ☐  Use of Upper Extremities       Intellectual:               │
│     ☐  Use of Lower Extremities          ☐  Coordination          │
│     ☐  Stamina                           ☐  Concentration         │
│                                                                   │
└─────────────────────────────────────────────────────────────────┘
```

The importance of planning in ergonomics is to define goals and objectify a process that develops an obvious set of procedures that result in solutions. In the systematic consideration of workers, ergonomics focuses attention on four aspects of human mechanics: how people move (biomechanics), how people use their senses, how people feel on the job (psychologically), and how people think. The idea is to reduce the risks of occupational illness and injury by planning an ergonomically fit safety program with a timeline and considerations for human resources and expense. Administrative procedures for purchasing and worker safety guidelines should be established. Worksite analysis should be done to determine and prioritize risks. Hazard engineering controls should be used to abate and reduce risks. Occupational health practitioners will provide medical management to help prevent and reduce lost work time and injury. And, finally, training must be conducted to help workers become their own safety and ergonomic analysists, contributing to the team effort that will turn ergonomic paper plans into workplace action plans.

22.1 Ergonomic Design Benefits

☐ Improved safety

☐ Legal compliance

22.2 Consequences of Not Using Ergonomic Design

☐ Lost time

☐ Increased cost

☐ Injury, illness

☐ Disease

☐ Fatality

☐ Legal citation

22.3 Sample of Planning a Project

Name	Scheduled Start Date	Scheduled Finish Date
Confirm team	10/03/97	10/14/97
Develop schedule	10/03/97	10/14/97
Establish fee budgets	10/03/97	10/14/97
Prepare questionnaire	10/17/97	10/21/97
Prepare presentation	10/17/97	10/21/97
Outline objectives & purpose	10/24/97	10/28/97
Obtain approval to proceed	10/24/97	10/28/97
Distribute questionnaire	10/24/97	10/28/97
Ten-year projections	10/31/97	11/07/97
Areas of potential change	11/14/97	11/18/97
Present statistics and data	11/21/97	11/25/97
Confirm results & conclusions	11/21/97	11/25/97
Presentation to board members	11/28/97	12/02/97

22.4 Ergonomic Approach to Architectural Design Planning

The process of sustaining a competitive edge through ergonomics provides tremendous opportunity for an organization. Yet it is just the first phase in a constant process of assessing strengths and weaknesses, making recommendations, and managing change.

22.4.1 Decision Making Process

☐ Take time to think about and plan who in the client organization will make the final decision on the recommended changes.

☐ A carefully chosen team of managers within the client organization should review the plan and its progress, as well as help sell it to senior management.

☐ Keep senior managers and other stakeholders involved at all times. If there are internal review committees, go over the plans with selected members before making formal presentations.

22.4.2 The Process Flow Chart

☐ Use a Critical Path Method (CPM) or Performance Evaluation and Review Technique (PERT) to create a process flow chart delineating the steps to be undertaken during the proposed change.

☐ Assign beginning and ending dates for all the process steps to be completed. The process from start to finish may involve hundreds of separate, discrete actions, including every meeting date, delivery, and decision.

☐ To help in this effort, a project manager should make sure that the logic is correct, and that the most critical parts of the process are properly identified.

- Prioritize opportunities.
- Identify customer needs, expectations, and goals
- Identify the product or service that is provided.
- Identify the department for each product or service and determine what department members consider to be important.
- Identify the capacity to provide design support for the product or service.

- Map the current process, and specify measurements
- Assess the process capability.
- Initiate a defect analysis, and determine actions to be taken.
- Define and document the process for doing the work.
- Document the improvement and set future target goals.
- Implement action.
- Mistake-proof the process and eliminate wasted efforts.
- Benchmark process.

☐ Plan on having at least six hours of team meetings a month, for twelve months, for all key people.

☐ Each team member will also need to prepare for two to ten hours before each meeting.

☐ Specialists from within or outside the organization may be needed to occasionally assist and to suggest new methods.

☐ The total cost of the first year's program alone could run well into six figures. With this sizable investment, it is imperative that upper management supports the project 100%.

22.5 Establishing a Vision

Establishing a vision of where to ultimately lead the organization is important, as is establishing a competitive edge and setting realistic goals.

☐ Allow the customer's input to affect the design process.

☐ Choose an architect well-versed in ergonomics. A well-prepared mission statement will then be a natural outgrowth.

☐ Determine and state why you are undertaking this process.

 - A suggested opening for the purpose statement would be: "We are undertaking this process of assessment and change to in order to maintain competitiveness and high performance in all areas of the safety management business."

☐ Establish early on a very strong customer relationship and emphasize the importance of employee involvement by indicating that "We will accomplish this by developing strong customer and vendor relationships and by involving our employees in all stages of data collection and decision making."

☐ State (and believe) that there are no preordained conclusions.

 - One way might be to adopt the following in the conclusion of the purpose statement: "This will be an open process leading to one of many possible, viable solutions."

22.6 User Enrollment

☐ User involvement in this process is important.

☐ The process of building a team is based on mutual trust and respect.

☐ People take more personal responsibility for higher quality and lower cost when they have as much knowledge, involvement, and choice as possible.

☐ Participation also deepens commitment and decreases rumors and misinformation.

The suggested essential steps in this process are:

☐ Announce the program in a formal meeting, with everyone from the entire organization present. Carefully explain the purpose of the program.

☐ Announce the results of each stage of the process to your employees.

☐ Involve everyone in the process of formally defining roles and responsibilities, focusing on the customer, work modeling, and measurement.

☐ Develop the capabilities of the employees to actively participate in each of these processes.

☐ Share the results with your employees; involve them in the process of fine tuning.

☐ Use every opportunity to discuss the process with everyone involved.

☐ It is important to recognize that all participants will be well aware that management is undertaking a serious effort to bring about change. It is best to share as much information as possible.

☐ Continue to evaluate all aspects of the business as it changes, and actively encourage all employees to support the progress.

☐ Sustaining the ergonomic edge is the first step in an evolutionary process that involves everyone in creating the type of organization they truly want.

☐ The greatest boon to developing a fully actuated, fully self-managed work group is the improvement of individual and team capabilities.

22.7 Focusing on the Customer

The most valuable lesson to learn is the importance of a systematic approach to focusing on the customer's requirements. This will result in the most benefits for employees as well as for customers.

☐ Establish the identities of your customers.

☐ Let them know that they are valuable customers.

☐ Learn precise customer requirements.

☐ Establish a clear connection between what they get and what they pay for.

☐ Sustain this effort for future improvement.

22.8 Work Modeling

As the above process unfolds, it becomes more apparent what the customer wants and what the employees are capable of providing.

☐ Maintain a purposeful decision-making procedure in order to evaluate the benefits (or liabilities) of alternative methods of providing facility services. This is especially true when it comes to evaluating in-house work forces vs. outsourcing options.

☐ Assess the skill level required to operate the facility, and the current resources or capabilities available to meet those needs, before any changes are made to the department organizational structure or teams.

☐ Decide whether to centralize or decentralize. This is called "work modeling" and there are numerous methodologies to do it. Here are some of the general steps to follow:

- Conduct an inventory of equipment and components.
- Prepare performance guidelines in conjunction with formal definition of roles and responsibilities.
- Determine work quantities.
- Conduct a risk assessment.
- Conduct a capability assessment.
- Recommend improvements and implementations.

22.8.1 Building Components

Develop specifications for all major building components.

☐ This requires an accurate inventory and condition assessment for all physical assets or major building components.

☐ A detailed inventory requires tremendous labor to initiate and maintain, but it does provide all the details needed.

☐ A focused performance guideline for each predictive, preventive, or routine work step must be provided for each building component or system.

☐ Each performance guideline needs to specify the purpose of the guideline, employee responsibilities, how often tasks are to be performed, the expectations of customers and facilities management, key drivers and measurement parameters, and how to measure success.

☐ After performance guidelines are determined, the quantity of work needing to be done at the facility is established. In other words, the service level, or frequency of occurrence is established.

☐ Cost factors can be included here, however avoid being sidetracked into a productivity issue (how quickly it can be done), rather than a quality issue of how long does it takes to do it right the first time (with zero defects).

☐ Using best practices and accepted industry standards, appropriate times can be allocated for each performance guideline.

22.8.2 Risk Assessment

Next, perform a relative risk assessment of all the services.

☐   This risk assessment needs to be performed from an overall business perspective, rather than from a facility perspective.

☐   It may be as simple as a subjective grading of high-medium-low risk or may involve establishing evaluation criteria with weighed factors on such issues as:

- strategic business alignment
- liability exposure
- internal culture
- security clearance
- operationally-critical processes

22.8.3 Skills and Capabilities Assessment

Next, perform a skills and capabilities assessment.

☐   This is best performed by a quality improvement team that can objectively decide if the required skills exist internally or externally.

☐   Another decision that can be made here is whether to embark on a training program to improve in-house skills (if they are deficient), or whether external work suppliers can provide greater benefits.

22.8.4 Grouping Facility Services

Next, decide how the facility services will be grouped—or if they will be grouped at all.

☐   Based on the volume of work, and the skills, capabilities and relative-risk assessments, a methodology of combining certain tasks can be established.

☐   A fairly simple method is to group all low-risk, low-skill and low-volume work together to establish "bundles" of work based on commonality. Several companies have decided to group all services together and consider them as one main bundle.

☐   The information gathered when bidding out services can be compared with the information gathered by benchmarking, to help establish what are an organization's performance capabilities.

Section 23

Safety

Human Factors to Be Considered

Biomechanical :
- ☐ Balance
- ☐ Coordination
- ☐ Sitting
- ☐ Standing
- ☐ Head Movement
- ☐ Lifting/Reaching
- ☐ Handling and Fingering
- ☐ Use of Upper Extremities
- ☐ Use of Lower Extremities
- ☐ Stamina

Sensory:
- ☐ Vision
- ☐ Hearing
- ☐ Olfactory
- ☐ Speech
- ☐ Skin

Psychological:
- ☐ Stress - Fatigue

Intellectual:
- ☐ Coordination
- ☐ Concentration

The ergonomic importance of safety is to reduce occupational illnesses and injuries by reducing the risks of accidents. An accident reduction strategy should include prevention strategies, such as prevention of accidents involving stored energy (electricity, torque, and chemicals). In addition, ergonomic plans should modify the rate of spatial distribution of energy in material handling by recommending appropriate equipment (e.g., better catwalks to access machines) and space divisions to locate resources closer to areas of use. Safety evaluations should include measuring the energy used in a space between people or inanimate objects. Safety evaluations should also consider what potential damage by people or damage to people could occur, such as the danger of slings that are used when frayed. Safety interventions include modification of contact surfaces and pinch points to prevent cuts, splinters, and bruises; strengthening the susceptible physical body with the correct use of personal protective equipment such as eyewear, hearing protection, and properly fitting gloves; minimizing the extent of loss or damage by immediate care for injured workers and maintenance of critical systems (fire sprinkler system and extinguishes); developing an immediate rehabilitation and light duty response to follow injuries, prevent lost time, and damage.

23.1 Ergonomic Design Benefits

- ☐ Improved safety

- ☐ Legal compliance

23.2 Consequences of Not Using Ergonomic Design

- ☐ Lost time

- ☐ Increased cost

- ☐ Injury, illness

- ☐ Disease

- ☐ Fatality

- ☐ Legal citation

- ☐ Lost quality

23.3 Ergonomic Design

☐   Beyond OSHA, ergonomic design should include fire protection, safety and water, safety of personnel, and environmental compliance.

23.4 Fire Protection

☐   The requirements for fire protection systems are stipulated in detail by local building codes. Most local codes are based on the model codes and recommendations of the National Fire Protection Association. As a result, model code information can safely be used to establish preliminary design budgeting.

☐   To correctly interpret the many model building code requirements and establish costing parameters, the building must first be classified. The following information is required to do so:

- fire zone
- occupancy group
- type of construction
- location of property
- number of occupants
- floor area

☐   With this information, systems can be purchased within the estimated budget. It is also important to review local code requirements to assess their impact on cost.

23.4.1 Standpipes

☐ In buildings where water may be used as the extinguishing agent, standpipes are often used to carry the water in large diameter pipes throughout the building.

☐ There are three standpipe systems that are recognized by the model codes: Dry, Wet, and Combination.

☐ Costing is based on building classification, number of floors, and floor-to-floor height.

23.4.2 Sprinklers

☐ Automatic sprinkler systems have been in use for many years in buildings as a very effective means for controlling and even extinguishing fires that are in the early stages.

- Being automatic, these systems do not require building occupants to activate them.
- The flow of water is comparable to a heavy rainfall.

☐ The model codes require automatic sprinkler systems in some buildings. In others, they are highly recommended. The most common types are:

- wet pipe
- firecycle
- dry pipe
- preaction

- deluge

☐ Sprinkler costing is based on building classification, floor area, and floor level.

23.5 Minimal Administrative Policies

☐ Safety training is required for all supervisors and employees.

23.6 Other Recommended Programs and Policies

☐ Accident prevention program

☐ Lockout/tagout program

☐ Respiratory protection program

☐ Hearing conservation program

☐ Chemical hygiene plan

☐ Hazard communication program

☐ Confined space program

☐ Emergency action plan

☐ Safety and health program

☐ Preventative maintenance program

☐   Assured equipment grounding conductor program

☐   Housekeeping plan

☐   Crane and derrick safety manual

☐   Medical surveillance program

☐   Ergonomics program

☐   Infection control program

☐   Written operation plan for emergency situations

☐   Bio-safety manual

☐   Work practices program

☐   Programs to comply with all substance-specific OSHA laws

☐   Programs for any other OSHA rule or state law that requires employers to adopt a written program

23.7   Safety of Personnel

☐   Safety programs protect operating personnel and property from preventable hazards.

- An example safety problem is refrigerant toxicity and flammability and potentially hazardous operating pressures and temperatures.

23.7.1 Applicable Standards

☐ Occupational Safety and Health Administration's (OSHA) 29 CFR Standards

☐ 29 CFRs 1910 and 1926

☐ American Society of Heating, Air Conditioning

☐ Refrigerating Engineers (ASHARE) Standard 15 (Safety Code for Mechanical Refrigeration)

☐ Standard 34 (Number Designation and Safety Classification of Refrigerants)

23.7.2 Essential Refrigerant Safety Program Aspects

☐ Material Safety Data Sheets (MSDSs) for documentation

☐ Chiller room sensing devices (refrigerant vapor detector/oxygen deprivation sensor)

☐ Sensor-activated alarm and ventilation system

☐ Self-contained breathing apparatus

☐ Automatic ventilation refrigerant evacuation system

☐ Relief and purge outdoor discharge piping

☐ Safe handling procedures for refrigerants

☐ Safe usage of recovery and reclaiming equipment

☐ General machinery room safety compliance

☐ General O & M safety awareness and practices

23.8 Environmental Compliance and Safety

What should environmental compliance include? Here are several relevant areas of interest at a typical non-manufacturing facility:

☐ Past history of environmental investigations or actions at the site (soil cleanups, asbestos abatement, interior air quality (IAQ) survey)

☐ Site conditions (topography, land use, geology)

☐ Potential problems from adjoining or nearby sites

☐ Underground or above-ground storage tank

☐ PCBs (transformers, capacitors, etc.)

☐ Asbestos-containing materials

☐ Air emissions from copying machines, print shops, etc.

☐ Sanitary or storm water discharges

☐ Registration of combustion equipment such as boilers and emergency generators

☐ Compliance with CFC regulations for maintenance and operation of air conditioning equipment

☐ Storage, use, and disposal of paints, solvents, batteries, and other hazardous materials

☐ Lead paint or lead in drinking water

☐ Interior air quality problems

23.9 Safety and Water

☐ Specify water purification systems for drinking fountains, break rooms, and cafeterias. These systems should be restaurant-quality purification units with replaceable cartridges.

☐ Water purification units should:

- Remove common off-tastes and odors, such as chlorine.
- Filter suspended particles as small as 0.5 microns.
- Reduce mineral and scale deposits in ice machines, coffee makers, and soda dispensers—reducing maintenance and increasing machine life

Section 24

Security

Human Factors to Be Considered	
Biomechanical :	**Sensory:**
☐ Balance	☐ Vision
☐ Coordination	☐ Hearing
☐ Sitting	☐ Olfactory
☐ Standing	☐ Speech
☐ Head Movement	☐ Skin
☐ Lifting/Reaching	**Psychological:**
☐ Handling and Fingering	☐ Stress - Fatigue
☐ Use of Upper Extremities	**Intellectual:**
☐ Use of Lower Extremities	☐ Coordination
☐ Stamina	☐ Concentration

The ergonomic importance of security is to consider the personal safety of employees in the workplace. The critical link of stress to increased workplace violence is well documented. Security relates to ergonomics, then, in the design of protected and secure spaces that reduce the stress to workers who may feel in danger or become endangered. The physical space of a workplace should create perceived zones of personal safety. It now very common practice to have limited access areas for workers who often work alone, either very late or in the very early morning hours. These workers also often request escorts when entering and leaving their work areas. Designs incorporate surveillance opportunities to "lonely" areas. The best surveillance opportunity is to watch spaces that are in the truncated U shape (as in looking over a balcony into a large lobby) versus spaces that form long rectangulars (as in offices with hundreds of panels forming office cubicles.) Safe zones should be reviewed with all workers to promote the relationship between worker safety and security.

24.1 Ergonomic Design Benefits

☐ Improved safety

☐ Legal compliance

24.2 Consequences of Not Using Ergonomic Design

☐ Lost time

☐ Increased cost

☐ Injury, illness

☐ Disease

☐ Fatality

☐ Legal citation

☐ Lost quality

24.3 Security Inspections

☐ Competent supervision and the ability to respond quickly and effectively to security needs are critical to maintaining high morale and effective security service.

☐ Security officers on the site should be supervised by experienced field officers and local management. Educational level and experience are important.

☐ Training should be specific to the site.

☐ Detailed regular inspection documentation should be provided.

☐ Security officers should be inspected each day.

- A daily report from each security officer—and special reports of unusual incidents observed by a security officer—should be submitted.

☐ On-site inspections should be conducted once a month at random by regional field officers or executive management.

☐ For a service problem, a response team from the security vendor should provide quick access to the complete chain of command, ranging from the on-site supervisor to corporate headquarters.

24.4 Security Services

☐ General investigations (overt or covert)

☐ Background screening of potential new employees

☐ Kidnapping and ransom insurance

☐ Security coverage for computers

☐ Security surveys of new facilities

☐ Preparation of a comprehensive security manual

☐ Electronic audio countermeasures sweeps

☐ Special publications of the latest prevention techniques

☐ Rapid development of strike or emergency personnel

☐ Anti-terrorist consulting

☐ Safety consulting

☐ Specialized personnel to support a broad range of security management activities

☐ Workplace violence consulting

Signage

Human Factors to Be Considered

Biomechanical :
- ☐ Balance
- ☐ Coordination
- ☐ Sitting
- ☐ Standing
- ☐ Head Movement
- ☐ Lifting/Reaching
- ☐ Handling and Fingering
- ☐ Use of Upper Extremities
- ☐ Use of Lower Extremities
- ☐ Stamina

Sensory:
- ☐ Vision
- ☐ Hearing
- ☐ Olfactory
- ☐ Speech
- ☐ Skin

Psychological:
- ☐ Stress - Fatigue

Intellectual:
- ☐ Coordination
- ☐ Concentration

Signs impact every aspect of job routines from informational (e.g., "Parking") to instructional (e.g., "Keep Guard Down") and are critical to maintaining safety (e.g., "Catwalk Off Limits"). Signs use visual, symbolic codes to communicate information. Well-designed signs directly convey their meaning. An example is a sign that forbids pedestrian traffic on a path intended for forklifts—a round sign with a line through the worker on the path denotes that the walkway is not for workers. An optimal sign does not have to be recoded or explained. Signs should be standardized throughout the organization to mean exactly the same thing wherever they appear. Signs should be relevant to the worker so that they are not ignored. Signs should always be placed in the visual field of all workers.

25.1 Ergonomic Design Benefits

☐ Improved safety

☐ Legal compliance

25.2 Consequences of Not Using Ergonomic Design

☐ Lost time

☐ Increased cost

☐ Injury, illness

☐ Disease

☐ Fatality

25.3 Legibility

☐ Use appropriate materials and methods for designing labels for specific environmental conditions. For instance, engraved labels should not be used in areas where dirt and debris might fill in the engraving.

☐ Proper protective coating of paper labels should be applied where corrosive chemicals or high abrasion are present.

☐ Labels may be made of other durable materials, including Tyvek™ or plastic.

☐ Install labels where they will not be damaged by routine operating or maintenance procedures.

☐ Labels inserted into permanently attached fixtures are preferable to those attached directly to equipment or walls. This makes labels easy to change as procedures and equipment change.

☐ Mount labels at an appropriate angle and use non-shiny materials to avoid glare, reflection, and shading.

☐ Tools or control devices requiring engraving on curved metal surfaces should have anodized surfaces to reduce spectral glare.

☐ Plan labeling for curved surfaces (such as piping on metal drums) so that all the lettering is readable from one viewing location.

☐ Use a border to improve readability of a single block of numbers or letters. Keep embellishments to a minimum. If several labels are clustered in the same area, put distinctive borders around the critical ones only.

☐ Use simple and decipherable typefaces.

☐ Use all capital letters for headings or messages of a few words only.

- Use upper and lower case letters for longer messages.
- Limit the use of *italics* to the emphasis of specific words or short phrases.
- An alternative method for emphasis is <u>underlining</u>.

☐ The minimum spacing between characters should be one stroke width.

☐ If a label is more than 79 inches above the floor where people are standing or sitting, character height should be increased in relation to width.

☐ Avoid the use of multicolored lettering. If colored print must be used in order to take advantage of color coding, legibility may be reduced.

In normal light (>10 foot-candles) conditions, letter and number size should follow these guidelines:

☐ Stroke width should be 1/6 of the letter height for black letters or numbers on a white background.

☐ Letter width should be 3/5 of the letter height (except "I" which should be one stroke width) and "M" and "W" which should be 4/5 of the height).

☐ Number width should also be 3/5 of the number height (except "1" which should be one stroke width).

☐ Characteristic features such as openings and counters should be obvious.

☐ The height is dependent on the viewing distance and the criticalness of the information.

In reduced-light areas (such as darkrooms), white letters on a black background are most visible. In this case, the stroke width should be 1/8 of the height.

25.4 Abbreviations

☐ Avoid abbreviations. If they must be used, use standard abbreviations.

☐ If a standard abbreviation does not exist, test the new abbreviation on inexperienced people to determine its understandability.

25.5 Information Coding

 Coded information is widely used in production systems. Some examples of coded information are:

- lot numbers
- part numbers
- product identification numbers
- invoice numbers
- operation sequences

☐ These numbers and/or letters can easily be misinterpreted, resulting in errors. The basic types of error are

- addition of characters
- substitution of characters
- transposition of characters

25.5.1 Information Coding Guidelines[1]

☐ Numeric codes are preferable to alphanumeric codes.

☐ Code length should not exceed 4 to 5 digits.

☐ If longer codes are necessary, the digits should be grouped in threes and fours and separated by a space or hyphen.

- Poor: 1234567
- Good: 123-4567

☐ If a numeric code system contains several digit sequences that re-occur very frequently, they should comprise the first or last section of the code.

- Poor: 35957
- Good: 59537

- Poor: 25952
- Good: 59522

☐ In tabular listings, when a digit sequence occurs repeatedly at the start of many-digit numbers, only the last digits for subsequent entries should be printed

- Poor: 7580170
- Good: 7580170

---

[1] Material from: Eastman Kodak Company, Ergonomic Design for People at Work, Volume 1, (New York: Van Nostrand Reinhold Co., 1983) p. 174-175.

- Poor: 7581010
- Good: 1010

- Poor: 7582030
- Good: 2030

- Poor: 7583040
- Good: 3040

- Poor: 7584050
- Good: 4050
- Poor: 7585060
- Good: 5060

- Poor: 7591000
- Good: 7591000

☐ Alphanumeric codes should have the letters grouped together rather than interspersed throughout the code.

- Poor: 7A8B4
- Good: AB784

☐ Use a specific location for numbers and letters to help avoid look-alike substitutions.

☐ Avoid the letters B, D, I, O, Q, and Z and the numbers 0, 1, and 8 in alphanumeric codes.

☐ Numbers should be used in the last few positions of long alphanumeric codes.

☐ Where possible, use pronounceable words and syllables instead of random letters.

- Poor: TGP32
- Good: TAC32

☐ Use simple typefaces with clearly distinguishable characters.

☐ Use bold printing and high contrast for all codes on labels and displays.

☐ Avoid faded characters on a card or sheet, especially if they must be read under low light conditions.

☐ Use color combinations that make codes easy to read.

☐ Avoid using 0 or 6 in codes when extensive handwriting is required.

☐ Characters should not be obliterated by keypunch holes.

Section 26

Storage

```
┌─────────────────────────────────────────────────────────────────────┐
│                    Human Factors to Be Considered                     │
│                                                                       │
│  Biomechanical :                        Sensory:                      │
│      ☐  Balance                             ☐  Vision                 │
│      ☐  Coordination                        ☐  Hearing               │
│      ☐  Sitting                             ☐  Olfactory             │
│      ☐  Standing                            ☐  Speech                │
│      ☐  Head Movement                       ☐  Skin                  │
│      ☐  Lifting/Reaching                Psychological:                │
│      ☐  Handling and Fingering              ☐  Stress - Fatigue      │
│      ☐  Use of Upper Extremities        Intellectual:                │
│      ☐  Use of Lower Extremities            ☐  Coordination          │
│      ☐  Stamina                             ☐  Concentration         │
│                                                                       │
└─────────────────────────────────────────────────────────────────────┘
```

The warehouse and storage areas are dynamic work areas and present important ergonomic considerations. Storage should not be a place for dumping potentially reusable items and retrieving them later. All storage activities need to be evaluated as potentially risky ones, where people are highly mobile, often operating forklifts, and dependent on critical tasks that require unobstructed vision of vertical planes. Assessment of storage spaces should include special considerations for storage from open storage using pallets stacked on the floor, automated high-risk bins, or cold storage where cold stress may occur. Hazardous material storage of gases, vapors, and dust requires specific and specialized methods. Life safety load reviews in case of emergency are critical to these storage areas. Shipping and receiving are activities where staging and coordination are critical to material movement from the dock, on and off trucks, or from railroad cars. Mobile racking on rail systems, although automated, has inherent risks from falling products. Ergonomic assessment and intervention of storage facilities and practices is important to understanding the interactions between the worker, materials, and equipment in an often fast-paced environment with many outside vendors.

26.1 Ergonomic Design Benefits

☐ Improved safety

☐ Legal compliance

26.2 Consequences of Not Using Ergonomic Design

☐ Lost time

☐ Increased cost

☐ Injury, illness

☐ Disease

☐ Fatality

26.3 Accommodation

☐ Storage areas should allow for maximum maneuverability and safety. For example, passages must be wide enough to allow easy access to resources.

☐ Reach and stamina are also critical concerns. For example, if closets have shelves or clothing rods that are too high, then a person in a wheelchair cannot retrieve or store things.

☐ Independent function is critical in order to maintain one's dignity and self-esteem.

- The degree of access to stored items can either foster or impede self-reliance.
- If storage areas are not accessible to all, additional staff must be made available to compensate for lack of reasonable accommodation.

☐ Storage areas should be accessible and uncluttered to allow independent access to supplies.

26.4 American Disabilities Act (ADA)—Storage—General

☐ It is required that all fixed storage facilities such as cabinets, shelves, closets, and drawers be accessible by ADA-AG 4.1.3(12) and 4.1.7 (3e) shall comply with 4.2.5.

26.4.1 Clear Floor Space

☐ A clear floor space at least 30 inches by 48 inches (760mm by 1220mm) and complying with 4.2.4, that allows either a forward or parallel approach by a person using a wheelchair, shall be provided at all storage facilities.

26.4.2 Height

☐ Accessible storage spaces shall be within at least one of the reach ranges specified in 4.2.5 and 4.2.6.

☐ Clothes rods shall be a maximum of 54 inches (1370mm) from the floor.

26.4.3 Hardware

☐ Hardware for accessible storage facilities shall comply with ADA-AG 4.2.7.4. Touch latches and U-shaped pulls are acceptable.

The figure below is an illustration of reach requirements and limits.

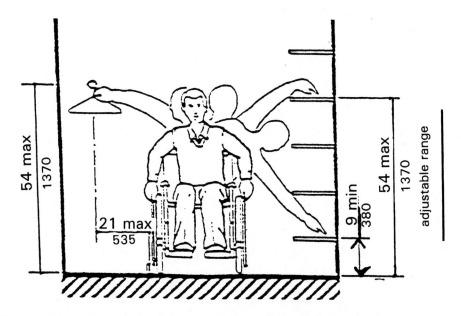

Figure 26-1. Reach Requirements for Storage Accessible to Individuals with Disabilities.

26.5 Shelving

☐ The design of storage areas should include shelving that allows access from a height of 29 inches above the floor, and does not exceed a shelf depth of 12 inches.

☐ There should be areas for individual storage and units for project maintenance.

☐ Shelving should allow flexibility, whether for the employees maintaining supplies and inventory, or for the customers who need access to products (e.g., a revolving display that allows a person access without movement).

26.5.1 Shelving Guidelines

☐ Reach should not be overhead or with fully extended arms.

☐ The weight of stored items should not exceed five pounds.

☐ There should be minimal vibration from adjacent equipment.

☐ No sharp edges should contact the hand or wrist.

☐ No finger or pinch grasp should be necessary.

☐ The access to an item should take no more than two minutes.

☐ The removal of an item should take no more than thirty seconds.

Section 27

Temperature

```
┌─────────────────────────────────────────────────────────────┐
│                 Human Factors to Be Considered               │
│                                                              │
│   Biomechanical :              Sensory:                      │
│      ☐  Balance                   ☐  Vision                  │
│      ☐  Coordination              ☐  Hearing                 │
│      ☐  Sitting                   ☐  Olfactory               │
│      ☐  Standing                  ☐  Speech                  │
│      ☐  Head Movement             ☐  Skin                    │
│      ☐  Lifting/Reaching       Psychological:                │
│      ☐  Handling and Fingering    ☐  Stress - Fatigue        │
│      ☐  Use of Upper Extremities Intellectual:               │
│      ☐  Use of Lower Extremities  ☐  Coordination            │
│      ☐  Stamina                   ☐  Concentration           │
│                                                              │
└─────────────────────────────────────────────────────────────┘
```

The egonomic importance of temperature control for employees working indoors is most often viewed as a comfort issue. However, as a condition of the work environment, temperature can significantly affect worker performance. As a rule of thumb, if the indoor temperature fluctuates up or down by more than 20 degrees from the best working temperature of 70 degrees, then ergonomic interventions for workers should be considered. It is important to develop a historical record of both existing and anticipated temperature conditions and worker reactions. With a record of actual temperature fluctuations and worker reactions, atmospheric controls can be developed to affect heating and cooling, air conditioning, circulation of air, humidity control, insulation, and shielding against radiation. For persons who are exposed to extreme conditions, clothing and protective gear is useful to extend the tolerance of workers. For example, screening workers for heat and cold stress tolerance is acceptable as long as it is part of the essential functions of the job (e.g., heat stress at a die cast machine). Additionally, workers should be gradually acclimatized—schedule work and rest breaks, rotate shifts, and modify work to reduce energy expenditure. It is critical to educate workers that hydration is necessary in order to maintain metabolism in all work conditions. NOTE: Thirst is not an adequate indication of water requirements.

27.1 Ergonomic Design Benefits

☐ Improved safety

☐ Legal compliance

27.2 Consequences of Not Using Ergonomic Design

☐ Lost time

☐ Increased cost

☐ Injury, illness

☐ Disease

☐ Fatality

27.3 Central Air System

☐ Provide adequate fresh air for percentage.

☐ Maintain humidification (30-50%) with maintenance.

☐   Use plants as humidifiers and oxygen generators.

27.4 Overhead Air Supply

☐   Use diffusers for occupancy/machine density.

☐   Regulate air speed and temperature controllers.

☐   Use directional controls to eliminate neck drafts.

☐   Lower partition height for fresh air distribution.

27.5 Underfloor Air Supply

☐   Condition the air of individual workspaces.

☐   Provide easy access to temperature controls.

☐   Reposition diffusers as necessary.

☐   Provide the ability to tie in furniture.

☐   Use an equipment-ducted floor for HVAC and telecommunications centers.

27.6 Individual Controls

☐   Allow for individual control of air speed and direction.

☐   Allow for individual control of air temperature.

☐ Have fresh air ducts near desks and individual workstations.

☐ Provide local air filtration (particulate and VOC).

☐ Provide local air monitoring devices.

☐ Install PC-based temperature sensors.

☐ Install radiant heat panels.

27.7 Cooling Demand

☐ A major concern in the modern electronic office is the greatly increased cooling demand that accompanies the increase in the amount of operational equipment. This demand is mostly generated by specific activities at specific times of day.

☐ It is not only energy inefficient, but also thermally uncomfortable, to adjust overall task-ambient air-conditioning setpoints to keep the hottest areas cool.

☐ Develop separate task and ambient cooling and ventilation systems, similar to the separation of task and ambient lighting. This requires establishing the differences between broadband ambient needs and time-and-activity-dependent task needs.

☐ The development of split task and ambient thermal air conditioning systems will require consideration of:

- terminal mixing boxes

- terminal reheat with closed-loop efficiency
- individual/local conditioning units
- multiple system cooling—air, water, radiant
- diffuser controls—density, location, volume, direction
- diffuser temperature mix (OA and RA)

27.8 Heat Loss/Heat Gain Control

☐ A major function of the building enclosure is the control of heat loss and heat gain through the enclosure and its openings.

☐ The effective detailing of the wall and roof sections for high R values, minimized thermal bridging, minimized air filtration and exfiltration, and moisture control is of critical concern not only for thermal comfort but also for structural integrity and air quality.

☐ The integration of enclosure and structure is key to heat loss/heat gain control, including the joining of facade/floor and column/beam.

☐ The detailing of openings to minimize thermal bridging and filtration, as well as to maximize component R values, has led to a wide range of new heat loss/gain control strategies.

- low E-glazings
- triple glazing, high R-value with high solar transmission
- new spacer technologies, gas-filled and vacuum air spaces
- thermal breaks, low-infiltration framing and hardware
- night insulation, air layers, foil layers
- transparent insulation

- wall and roof insulation, details to minimize thermal bridging, air filtration, moisture migration
- enclosure and structure integration
- waste heat and solar heat dumping in the facade

27.9 Passive and Active Solar Heating

☐ Solar and other passive heating concepts are most applicable in buildings where heating is the predominant energy load, and there are often viable uses for solar heating in offices.

☐ Thermosiphoning air panels or phase-change panels can offset perimeter loads.

☐ Solar energy through direct gain, indirect gain, or isolated gain can be used to meet the heating needs in greenhouse and atrium areas, which provide healthy spaces for plants, and rest areas for office workers with sunlight, increased oxygen, and vegetation.

☐ The availability of photovoltaic cells for solar power generation is a major opportunity for supporting tomorrow's power-hungry office; and the replacement of electric lighting with innovative fiber optics is well within our energy future.

27.10 Enclosure Integrity

☐ Besides meeting the thermal, visual, and air quality needs, the enclosure must also be designed for long term durability.

☐ Enclosure integrity can be defined as the protection of the building's facade and contents from damage due to physical chemical, or thermal forces or loads, including those due to moisture, temperature changes, air movement, radiation, biological incursion, and man-made or natural disasters.

☐ A number of factors affect the long-term integrity of facades.

- module dimensions and assembly
- finish material
- compatibility of materials (phosphorescence, streaking)
- continuity of the "rainscreen"
- critical separations between the continuous rainscreen, thermal barrier, and vapor barrier

☐ Be aware that the desire to solve each of these problems in a single line of defense has led to countless building facade failures.

☐ The introduction of new enclosure components and assemblies must take into account the following critical aspects, and also improve the long-term maintainability and durability of facades.

- innovative waterproofing, detailing, drainage, and on-site water management
- continuous vapor barrier techniques
- thermal break materials; structure and enclosure connection
- high-integrity expansion materials
- rainscreen technologies, vented facades
- built-in sensors, "tattletales" for mechanical and thermal properties
- fire and smoke management components and assemblies

☐ Enclosure must enable water conservation and reuse.

☐ Effective water collection on the building and rerouting past the facade for gray water use in landscaping, will not only conserve fresh water resources (limited in many areas), but also will enhance the long-term durability of the enclosure.

Section 28

Tools

Human Factors to Be Considered

Biomechanical :
- ☐ Balance
- ☐ Coordination
- ☐ Sitting
- ☐ Standing
- ☐ Head Movement
- ☐ Lifting/Reaching
- ☐ Handling and Fingering
- ☐ Use of Upper Extremities
- ☐ Use of Lower Extremities
- ☐ Stamina

Sensory:
- ☐ Vision
- ☐ Hearing
- ☐ Olfactory
- ☐ Speech
- ☐ Skin

Psychological:
- ☐ Stress - Fatigue

Intellectual:
- ☐ Coordination
- ☐ Concentration

The ergonomic importance of tools is to reduce the physical workload on the employee and to prevent occupational illness and injury. Tools need to be able to perform their function while being compatible with the anthropomorphic and biomechanical characteristics of workers.

28.1 Ergonomic Design Benefits

☐ Improved safety

☐ Legal compliance

28.2 Consequences of Not Using Ergonomic Design

☐ Lost time

☐ Increased cost

☐ Injury, illness

☐ Disease

☐ Fatality

28.3 Ergonomic Approach to Tools

☐ A successful ergonomics program must include many other facets besides the use of ergonomically designed tools. These include:

- injury management
- ergonomic analysis of existing and proposed jobs
- training in ergonomics at all work levels
- implementation of many engineering and administrative changes

☐ When a comprehensive ergonomics program is in place, the benefits will clearly justify the investment.

- of reduced incidence and severity of injuries
- decreased medical and workers' compensation costs
- reduced lost time
- improved productivity

□   The cost of acquiring ergonomically designed tools initially may be higher than for purchasing standard tools. The increased benefits far outweigh the extra costs.

□   Tools that are ergonomically designed diminish the risk of cumulative trauma injuries such as Carpal Tunnel Syndrome and tendinitis. As part of a complete ergonomics program, these tools save money in many ways, including:

- medical costs—doctor visits, therapy and surgery
- workers' compensation costs
- lost and restricted workdays
- cost of retraining injured employees
- cost of training new employees to take jobs of injured employees

□   Additionally, jobs that cause cumulative trauma injuries often produce some of the following problems:

- high absenteeism
- high turnover
- low employee morale
- frequent rest breaks
- high material waste
- poor work quality and decreased production rates

28.4 Biomechanics of the Hand and Wrist

In order to understand why these cumulative trauma disorders occur so frequently, and how to prevent them, it is necessary to first understand the biomechanics of the wrist and hand.

Briefly, it is important to realize that the thumb is controlled by strong, short muscles in the hand. In contrast, the fingers are controlled by tendons that pass through the hand and wrist into the forearm, where they attach to muscles. These tendons, some blood vessels, and the Median nerve (which feeds the thumb, index finger, middle finger and part of the ring finger) pass through the carpal tunnel in the wrist. This tunnel is an arch formed by small bones with a ligament stretched across them. Cumulative trauma injuries may occur when these tendons, blood vessels, and nerves become impinged upon by repetitive use or by awkward hand and wrist postures and movements.

28.5 Cause of Cumulative Trauma Injuries

☐   Tendinitis

- more than 2,000 manipulations per hour
- single or repetitive local strain
- forceful and rapid repetitive movements
- work with a deviated wrist, especially when combined with forceful exertions of the thumb
- exertions with a flexed wrist

☐   Carpal Tunnel Syndrome

- work with repetitive wrist flexion or extreme extension, especially in combination with a pinch grip
- repeated force on the base of the palm or wrist

28.6 Reducing Cumulative Trauma Injuries

☐ The four major steps that should be taken to reduce the incidence and severity of cumulative trauma injuries are:

- use anthropometric data
- reduce the frequency of repetitions
- reduce the force required
- eliminate awkward postures

28.6.1 Anthropometry

☐ Anthropometry is the study of human body dimensions. It is important to consider the varying body dimensions of workers in order to select tools to fit their physical capabilities.

☐ Ergonomist aim to accommodate 90 percent of the population, those between the 5th and 95th percentiles.

☐ When designing and selecting tools, anthropometric data should be used to provide tools that are comfortable for all users and will not cause injuries.

☐ This data is useful when determining handle length, grip span, tool weight, and other pertinent factors.

28.6.2 Reduce the Frequency of Repetitions

☐ Tasks that require high repetition rates require more muscle effort and less recovery time, which can lead to fatigue and injury.

Researchers are beginning to determine acceptable or safe limits for repetition.

☐   Reduce the number of repetitions as much as possible by:

-   broadening the variety of tasks each employee performs
-   rotating employees
-   encouraging employees to take mini-breaks and perform relief exercises
-   limiting overtime
-   increasing number of employees assigned to a particular task

28.6.3 Reduce the Force Required

☐   If the force requirements are too high, the soft tissues may be strained, causing injury.

☐   Additionally, tendons, blood vessels, and nerves are impinged upon when the wrist is held in contact with hard or sharp-edged surfaces.

☐   Force on the hand should be reduced as much as possible by:

-   using power tools and assists whenever possible
-   using the stronger whole-hand grip instead of the weaker pinch grip
-   spreading the force over a wide area
-   providing adequate gripping surfaces that are not slippery, sharp, or excessively hard

28.6.4 Eliminate Awkward Postures

☐ Jobs should not require employees to work with awkward postures that impose biomechanical stresses on the joints and tissues, causing injuries.

☐ The following steps may be taken to eliminate awkward postures:
- keep wrist in a neutral position
- keep elbow close to the body and bent 90-100°
- avoid reaching above shoulder height or behind the body
- minimize forearm rotation

28.7 Selecting the Correct Tool

As already indicated, improper tool selection or misuse of tools can cause cumulative trauma disorders. When selecting a tool, it is important to consider the tool design and what postures are required to do the task.

The following ergonomic guidelines are helpful in acquiring tools to perform specific functions:

☐ Grip forces should be distributed over as wide an area as possible, and should not be concentrated on one or two fingers or in the center of the palm, which can lead to tendinitis or carpal tunnel syndrome.

☐ Choose tools with handles that span the hand and extend beyond the palm.

☐ Tools should not require employees to use the pinch grip. Maintaining the pinch grip, such as when holding tweezers or small components, forces the fingers to work four or five times harder than when gripping with the entire hand. The pinch grip combined with wrist deviation can lead to carpal tunnel syndrome.

☐ Select a tool that can be held with the entire hand.

☐ The tool handle should not exert forces on the sides of the fingers and the hand should not be exposed to sharp edges or corners. This is important since nerves and blood vessels are close to the skin and can be easily damaged.

☐ Select tools with rounded edges at all areas of potential contact.

☐ If the employee will be putting his/her fingers inside the handle, such as when using scissors or handsaws, be sure there is ample room for the fingers and hand.

☐ If the user will be wearing gloves, be sure there is sufficient clearance for the glove thickness.

☐ There should be no finger grooves in the handles of tools. These grooves do not accommodate a wide range of hand sizes and the fingers can rest on the edges of the grooves, increasing the risk of nerve or blood vessel damage.

☐ A tool with knurled or textured gripping surfaces will be easier to hold and will reduce grip force requirements without causing injury.

☐ Handles should be covered with smooth, no-slip, and compressible material. This allows the hand to avoid exerting unnecessary force to hold a slippery tool in place. However, be sure the covering is not so soft that debris could become embedded.

☐ Additionally, handles that are too soft diminish the feedback to the hand, which may result in excessive pressure being exerted to complete the task.

☐ Choose a tool that can be used with both the right and left hands. It is not practical to have both right-handed and left-handed tools, because they are often held in the wrong hand or in the wrong configuration, which can lead to discomfort or injury.

☐ Select tools that will allow the wrist to be held straight. Each job function may require different wrist positioning, which would necessitate the use of more than one tool for the job. Work performed with unnatural deviated wrist postures can lead to tendinitis or Carpal Tunnel Syndrome.

☐ Choose tools that will allow the elbows to be held close to the body. Working with raised elbows can cause muscle fatigue and pain.

28.7.1 Specific Guidelines for Pliers and Cutters

☐ Handle length should be at least 4.0 inches.

☐ Grip span should be 3.0-4.5 inches (open) and 2.0-2.5 inches (closed).

☐ Select tools with spring returns.

☐ Select tools with no finger grooves.

☐ Handle curvature of no more than 0.5 inches over its entire length; handles should be almost straight with only slight curves.

☐ The high points of the curves should rest in the center of the palm and against the middle part of the fingers.

☐ Each handle of the tool should be a mirror image of the other handle. This allows the tool to be comfortably and safely held in a variety of configurations.

☐ Tools should not have right- and left-handed models.

☐ A tool should only be used for the job for which it was designed. Using it for other jobs may increase the risk of injury.

☐ Select only high quality tools that will do the job for extended periods of time in the best manner possible.

- This will allow employees to perform their jobs more safely and efficiently and reduce the chance of tools breaking.

EXAMPLE:
Cutters and saws should have the highest quality blades that will maintain their sharpness, and not require an increase of force over time, as does a tool whose blade becomes dull.

28.7.2 Specific Guidelines for Power Tools

☐   Handle breadth should be 2.0-3.0 inches for pistol-grip tools.

☐   Handle diameter should be 2.0-2.5 inches for cylindrical tools.

☐   Handle length should be at least 4.0 inches.

☐   Finger-stop flange should be at the base of pistol-grip tools.

☐   There should be no finger grooves on the tool.

☐   Handle should be located near tool's center of gravity.

☐   Use an overhead balancer with heavy tools (> 1.0 lb.).

☐   Push-to-start activation should be used whenever possible.

☐   Thumb triggers and strip triggers are preferred over single button triggers.

☐   Minimize exposure to the vibration of power tools by selecting a tool with compressible rubber handles.

☐   If necessary, provide padded gloves, interject rest periods, or follow a job rotation schedule.

☐   Select tools with torque-control settings whenever applicable.

☐ All power and air cords should be very flexible and not interfere with the operation and handling of the tool.

28.7.3 Specific Guidelines for Manual Screwdrivers

☐ Handles should be at least 5.0 inches long.

☐ Handle diameter of medium and large blade screwdrivers that are used to exert force should be in the range of 1.0-1.35 inches, indicating a recommended circumference of 3.1-4.2 inches.

☐ Handle diameter of small thin-blade screwdrivers that are used for precision operations should be in the range of 0.7-0.8 inches, translating into a circumference of 2.2-2.5 inches.

☐ There should be a flange on the base of the handle. This will reduce the risk of slippage and decrease the grip-force requirements.

☐ Choose a tool that does not have fluted handles, finger grooves, or large indentations on the handles. These should be avoided because they can cause discomfort and nerve and blood vessel damage.

28.7.4 The Final Selection Process

☐ When selecting new ergonomically designed tools, it is important to choose 1-3 possible tools and evaluate each one very carefully.

- The evaluation should include a visual check to determine which ergonomic criteria are met.

☐ Most importantly, the tools should be used and evaluated by a representative group of employees for an extended period of time (at least two weeks).

☐ Each employee who uses the tools should complete a written survey to provide information on worker comfort and tool performance levels. Once all the data have been collected and analyzed, new tools can be selected.

28.8 Training

☐ After purchasing ergonomically designed tools, all employees who will use them should receive proper training.

☐ Training should include an introduction to ergonomic principles as well as specific instructions on how to correctly use the tools.
   - It is often difficult for employees to get used to a new tool or method, but it's even more difficult if nothing is explained or demonstrated.

☐ All the benefits of purchasing new ergonomically designed tools can be destroyed if they are not properly introduced into the workplace.

28.9 Tool Maintenance

☐ An organized and thorough tool maintenance program is essential. The ergonomic benefits of a tool can be negated if it is not working properly.

☐ All cutting blades should be sharpened when they begin to dull. Using a dull blade requires the employee to exert more force to complete a task than when using a sharp blade.

☐ Torque levels should be checked regularly to ensure that they are appropriate. Using a tool with the wrong torque can make it difficult to complete the task and can cause the tool to twist in the hand, forcing the wrist to overextend quickly.

☐ In addition, springs on two-handled tools such as pliers and cutters must be working well. Tools without properly working springs require the employees to open the tool with their inlays after each use.

☐ And finally, tools with defects such as worn handles and broken parts should be replaced immediately.

Section 29

Windows

Human Factors to Be Considered

Biomechanical :
- ☐ Balance
- ☐ Coordination
- ☐ Sitting
- ☐ Standing
- ☐ Head Movement
- ☐ Lifting/Reaching
- ☐ Handling and Fingering
- ☐ Use of Upper Extremities
- ☐ Use of Lower Extremities
- ☐ Stamina

Sensory:
- ☐ Vision
- ☐ Hearing
- ☐ Olfactory
- ☐ Speech
- ☐ Skin

Psychological:
- ☐ Stress - Fatigue

Intellectual:
- ☐ Coordination
- ☐ Concentration

The importance of windows to ergonomics is to consider that windows still represent a symbol of higher status and freedom between the "haves versus the have nots" and, therefore, windows present a psychological feeling of control. The dominant opinion among workers in windowless environments is that they are being deprived of both natural light and "real" air. This deprivation, then, appears to be a psychological one. Workers often add, "I am trapped in here." This is particularly true in climates where weather keeps people indoors for many weeks. The real data varies from industry to industry as to whether or not windowed environments increase productivity and quality. It appears that more workers than not desire windows as a psychological lift or break. Yet, as always, individuals vary in their preferences, attitudes, and aesthetic impressions.

29.1 Ergonomic Design Benefits

☐ Improved safety

☐ Legal compliance

29.2 Consequences of Not Using Ergonomic Design

☐ Lost time

☐ Increased cost

☐ Injury, illness

☐ Disease

☐ Fatality

29.3 Solar Control

☐ Solar control will be the second most important function of the enclosure in tomorrow's office, since both solar overheating and glare control are significant concerns in the electronic workplace.

☐ A number of existing and emerging enclosure components and assemblies deal directly with the following concerns.

- low-heat gain, high-light gain glass
- glazings for high sun-angle reflection, low sun penetration

- interior shading devices—blinds, roll-down reflecting/ diffusing screens
- exterior shading devices—blinds, roll-down screens, overhangs, awnings, vegetation, glazing louvers
- integral shading devices—slimshades with air extract, dynamic electrochromic glazings, photochromic glazings
- vented enclosures—rainscreens, double roofs
- mechanical penthouse shading, air-intake shading

29.3.1 Solar Overheating

☐ The quick response to solar overheating is to reduce window surface area and use highly reflective glass.

- This reaction, however, has severe consequences, removing office workers from light, view, outdoor contact, and sense of season and time of day (Even plants suffer under these conditions).
- In addition, this response creates increased brightness contrast problems at the perimeter, creating "bright holes in a dark field".

29.3.2 Glazings

☐ Utilize glazings that provide high reflectivity without diminishing light gain and view, thereby incorporating the best thermal and visual qualities in a single component (e.g., Azurlite™, Frit™).

☐ Glazings that offer clear views and high light gain can be combined with interior or exterior shading devices, such as diffusing screens or blinds, to provide more options and give even better long-term energy performance.

Section 30

Summary

30.1 The Safety Manager's Role in Integrating Ergonomics with Project Management

Safety managers should promote ergonomics in order to:

- ☐ Create opportunity.

- ☐ Widen exposure.

- ☐ Secure special assignments.

- ☐ Facilitate consideration of ergonomics at high level meetings.

They should:

- ☐ Provide current information.

- ☐ Create learning opportunities.

- ☐ Hold "What if?" sessions.

- ☐ Ask, "What would you do in this situation?"

- ☐ Provide greater access to resources.

- ☐ Criticize when appropriate and constructive

30.2 Key Issues for Success

A safety management ergonomics program has to address and resolve many complicated ergonomic issues:

☐ Commitment and attitude of upper management

☐ Relevance of program to department, division, and corporate goals at any given point in time

☐ Flexibility of implementation methods

☐ In-house accounting, procurement, inventory, and distribution processes versus budget and implementation requirements

☐ Overall financial condition of company

☐ Overall financial priority of ergonomics versus other safety program

☐ Workload of employees who are responsible for implementing ergonomics requirements

Table 30-1. Disability Factors by Laws				
Factors	ATBCB	ADAAG	ANSI	Title(s)
ACCESSIBILITY:				
Accessible Route	1190.60	4.3	–	I, II, III
Parking/Passenger Zones	1190.60	4.6	–	I, II, III
Curb Ramp	1190.70	4.8, 4.9	–	I, II, III
Ramps/Stairs	1190.70	4.8, 4.9	–	I, II, III
Elevators/Platforms	1190.100	4.10, 4.11	–	I, II, III
Drinking Fountains	1190.160	4.15	–	I, II, III
Restrooms	1190.150	4.16 – 4.24	–	I, II, III
ADAPTABILITY:				
Protruding Objects	–	4.4	–	I, II, III, IV
Controls/Operator Mechanics	1190.170	4.27	–	I, II, III, IV
Door Handles	1190.170	4.20, 4.16	A117.1	I, II, III, IV
COMFORT:				
Seating	–	4.32	–	I
COMMUNICATION:				
Telephones	1190.210	4.31	A117.1	I, II, III, IV
DENSITY:				
Wheelchair Turning Space	–	4.2	–	I, III
DIVISION OF SPACE:				
Assembly Areas	–	4.33	7.1	I
Service Counters	–	7.2	7.1	I
EQUIPMENT:				
Keyboards/Reachers	–	–	–	I
FINISHES:				
Ground/Floor Surface	–	4.5	–	I, II, III

Table 30-1 continued				
FURNITURE:				
Tables/Work Surface	–	4.32	–	I, III
IMAGE:				
Environmental Setting	–	–	–	I, II
LIGHTING:				
Independent Task Lighting	–	–	–	I, II, III
MAINTENANCE:				
Service Contracts	–	–	–	I
NOISE:				
Sound Reduction Panels	–	–	–	I, II, III, IV
PASSAGES:				
Doors	1190.13	4.13	–	I, II, III
Entrances	1190.120	4.14	–	I, II, III
Tactile Cues	1190.190	4.29	–	I, II, III
SAFETY:				
Alarms	–	4.20	–	I, II, III, IV
SIGNAGE:				
International Signage	1190.20	4.30	–	I, II, III
STORAGE:				
Fixed Storage	1190.170	4.25	–	I
TEMPERATURE/AIR QUALITY				
Air Conditioning/Heating	–	–	–	III
TRAINING:				
Ergonomic Training	–	–	–	I, III
WINDOWS:				
Doubled Pane Glass	1190.140	4.12	–	I

30.3 The World of Safety Management and Ergonomics

☐ The world of safety management is changing, and with it the demands of form and function to involving human factor and work.

30.3.1 Demographic and Legal Changes

Demographic and legal changes are requiring organizations to act more humanistically

☐ The growing labor shortage will require corporations to recruit people who did not work in the 1980s, and to creatively retain and redeploy existing labor.

☐ This accelerated change is pushing organizations to use self-managed work teams and inter-disciplinary product development teams to avoid delays in making decisions.

☐ The U.S. labor supply will increase less than 1% per year, the slowest growth since the 1940s. The late 1990s will bring the tightest labor market in decades.

☐ Because of the increasing labor shortage, corporations will recruit people who did not work in the 1980s (e.g., in the U.S., 3.3 million people who took early retirement, child labor, and the 14 million nonworking women caring for families).

☐ Job sharing programs are offered by 16% of U.S. companies.

30.3.2 Legal Authorities

☐   Regulatory agencies

- Department of Labor
- Department of Transportation
- Environmental Protection Agency
- Department of Health and Human Services
- National Institute for Occupational Safety and Health
- Occupational Safety and Health Administration

☐   Regulatory acts and laws

- The Americans with Disabilities Act
- The Clean Air Act
- The Clean Water Act
- Federal Insecticide, Fungicide, and Rodenticide Act Federal Railroad Safety Act
- Flammable Fabrics Act
- Hazardous Materials Transportation Act
- The National Energy Policy Act
- The Noise Control Act
- Poison Prevention Packaging Act
- The Ports and Waterways Safety Act
- Resource Conservation and Recovery Act
- Toxic Substance Control Act

30.3.3 Economic Parameters

Architects are subject to increasingly stringent economic parameters.

☐ In 1989, there were 14.6 million full-time, home-based businesses in the U.S. By 1995, there will be 20.7 million.

☐ Computers are turning structures into "smart" buildings that monitor and run themselves—and connect occupants with the rest of the world.

- Mitsubishi Real Estate connected twenty-two buildings in Tokyo's Marunouchi district with a network of optic fibers. If enough smart buildings are interconnected, a "smart city" will be created, which can be linked to other smart cities of the future.

☐ In 1985, an average of 18 million Americans—one of every six workers—were working part-time.

30.3.4 Technological Change, Compressed Product Cycles, and Global Competition

The major themes of the 1990s are technological change, compressed product cycles, and global competition.

☐ Between 1970 and 1986, the number of people employed by temporary-help firms grew from 184,000 to 760,000.

☐ Flexible work schedules were available to 13.6% of the workforce in 1985.

☐ Almost nine million workers—one out of every twelve—were spending at least eight hours per month working at home during normal work hours.

30.3.5 Telecommunications

☐ Improved telecommunications permits us to do business from home with a Tokyo office or a rural location in Indiana, almost as if we are sitting across a table, sharing conversation and documents.

☐ New technologies have changed the importance of scale and location and have extended the power of the individual.

Table 30-2. Projected Growth Rate by Occupation			
	1984	2000	% Change
Total Employment	106, 843 (K)	122, 760 (K)	14.9%
Executive/Administrative Managerial	10.6 %	11.2 %	22.1 %
Professional Workers	12.0 %	12.7 %	21.7 %
Technicians and Support	3.0 %	3.4 %	28.7 %
Salesworkers	10.5 %	10.9 %	19.9 %
Administrative Support/Clerical	17.5 %	16.7 %	- 9.5 %
Private Household Workers	0.9 %	0.7 %	- 18.3 %
Service Workers	14.6 %	15.4 %	21.3 %
Production, Craft, Repair	11.4 %	11.1 %	11.7 %
Operators/Fabricators/Labor	16.2 %	15.2 %	7.3 %
Farming/Forestry/Fisheries	3.3 %	2.8 %	- 3.0 %
PERCENT OF WORKFORCE	100.0 %	100.1 %	–

☐ Computers, cellular phones, and fax machines (9 million) empower individuals and make them more productive and efficient.

☐ Groupware—a new type of software (IBM-TeamFocus, Lotus-Notes, Ventana-Group Systems, Collaborative Technologies-VisionQuest) is linking departments and colleagues in different locations to improve the efficiency, quality, and speed of collaborative projects.

30.3.6 Education

☐ One-quarter of the workforce aged 25 to 64 consists of college graduates or higher, twice the amount of twenty years ago.

☐ Another 20% have had one to three years of college, more than double the old amount. That means nearly half—about 45%—of the workforce is college educated. In addition, 40% are high school graduates. That leaves just 15% who are adult age without a high school diploma. Twenty years ago, 41% had not completed high school.

Safety managers faced with all of these demographic and physical changes and challenges must be creative in designing new work environments.

Appendix A

Framework of an Ergonomics Plan as Proposed by Definitions Included in OSHA and Cal-OSHA Regulations

The essential components of an Ergonomics Plan include the following:

1. A WRITTEN PLAN defining resources, policies and procedures for ergonomics includes

   - ☐ Mission statement
   - ☐ Comprehensive management procedures documenting a systematic plan
   - ☐ Goals and objectives with timelines
   - ☐ Guidelines for management commitment of personnel and resources
   - ☐ Guidelines for employee involvement
   - ☐ Guidelines for risk analysis
   - ☐ Guidelines for control measures
   - ☐ Guidelines for medial management
   - ☐ Guidelines for on-going feedback
   - ☐ Guidelines for accountability
   - ☐ Guidelines related to production standards
   - ☐ Guidelines related to quality

2. ADMINISTRATIVE CONTROLS to the plans commitment is communicated in writing to define responsibilities, expectations and accountability of everyone in the workplace. Policies identify responsibility of the worker,

supervisor, safety manager, human resources department, insurance represent-atives, and treating medical professionals for effective worker interactions

- ☐ Management actions
- ☐ Management commitment
- ☐ Management resources
- ☐ Management motivation
- ☐ Management authority
- ☐ Management accountability

3. WORK SITE ANALYSIS to identify (high, medium, low) occupational risks for cumulative trauma disorders

- ☐ Examine injury records
- ☐ Examine trends
- ☐ Develop a risk list upon which corrective actions are prioritized
- ☐ Examination of the worksite by a qualified ergonomics professional
- ☐ Identification of hazards an conditions creating ergonomic risks
- ☐ Examine work procedures
- ☐ Examine work environments
- ☐ Examine work habits
- ☐ Examine tools and instruments
- ☐ Examine materials
- ☐ Examine machines and equipment

4. ERGONOMIC HAZARD PREVENTION AND CONTROLS to eliminate identified risks. Controls by training of supervisors and workers, enforcement of safe work practices, worker self-care procedures, and appropriate medical management to include early problem intervention and aggressive return-to-work

☐   Abate the identified ergonomic hazards in a timely manner

☐   Controls by modification in work design

☐   Controls by work assignment

☐   Controls by work procedures

☐   Controls by exposure reduction

☐   Tools and instruments

☐   Machines and equipment

☐   Materials

☐   Environment

5.   EFFECTIVE MEDICAL MANAGEMENT to encourage optimum problem recovery with specific policies addressing early problem reporting, treatment protocols and restricted duty

☐   Early recognition of symptoms with effective early treatment

☐   Effective case management policies

☐   Effective return-to-work strategies

6.   SAFETY AND HEALTH TRAINING for mangers, supervisors and employees—supervisors are trained to identify and address ergonomic risks they may encounter in work design or worker behavior. Employees are educated and motivated to participate in self-protection and fatigue avoidance procedures

☐   To build worker skills in job safety analysis

☐   To build skills to correct ergonomic hazards and work practices

7.   LONG-TERM IMPLEMENTATION, FEEDBACK AND REVIEW to assess progress and assure long-range implementation—all components of the ergonomics plan include accountability for implementation, ongoing assessment of effectiveness and identification of new problems.

- ☐ Ergonomic team leader appointed
- ☐ Ergonomic team formed
- ☐ Employee input procedures in place
- ☐ Annual review and update of objectives and actions
- ☐ Corrective actions have dates of implementation
- ☐ Public relations strategy
- ☐ Evaluation of effects
- ☐ Workplace is monitored for ongoing problems
- ☐ Injury claim trends monitored
- ☐ Job analyses by an ergonomics team
- ☐ OSHA-200 reviews
- ☐ Employee suggestion mechanisms
- ☐ Goals review annually

Appendix B

Proposed Definitions for California General Industry Safety Orders

Article 106, Ergonomics

Section 5110, Repetitive Motion Injuries

☐ The section shall apply to a job, process, or operation of identical work activity at the workplace where repetitive motion injuries (RMIs) occur after [OAL to fill in effective date]. For Purposes of this section, RMIs are injuries resulting from a repetitive job, process, or operation of identical work activity at the workplace that have been the predominant cause of a diagnosed, objectively identified musculoskeletal injury to more than one employee within the last 12 months. A licensed physician shall perform the diagnosis of a RMI. For definitional purposes predominant means 50% or more of the injury was caused by a repetitive job, process or operation of identical work activity.

☐ Exemption: Employers with 9 or fewer employees.

☐ Every employer subject to this section shall establish and implement a program designed to minimize RMIs. The program shall include:

- worksite evaluation
- control of exposures which have caused RMIs and training of employees

☐ Worksite evaluation. Each job, process, or operation of identical work activity covered by this section or a representative number of such jobs. Processes or operations of identical work activities shall be evaluated for exposures that have caused RMIs.

☐ Control of exposures that have caused RMIs. Any exposures that caused RMIs shall, in a timely manner, be corrected, or if not capable of being corrected, minimized to the extent feasible. The employer shall consider engineering controls such as work station redesign, adjustable fixtures or tool redesign, and administrative controls such as job rotation, work pacing or work breaks.

☐ Training: Employees shall be provided training that includes an explanation of:

- the employer's program;
- the exposures which have been associated with RMIs;
- the symptoms and consequences of injuries caused by repetitive motion;
- the importance of reporting symptoms and injuries to the employer; and
- methods used by the employer to minimize RMIs

Appendix C

Summary of Key Provisions of the Regulatory Text Draft Ergonomic Protection Standard

Approach

- ☐ Organize the standard for ease of reference.
- ☐ Provide user-friendly text wherever possible.
- ☐ Supply compliance assistance material.
- ☐ Use performance-orientations.
- ☐ Remember to consider accommodations for small employers.

Scope and Application

- ☐ Problem affects broad spectrum of workers and industries
- ☐ Tiered approach—use of signal risk factors to target jobs for further evaluation
- ☐ Signal risk factors are:

  - performance of same motion or pattern every few seconds for more than 2-4 hours at a time
  - fixed or awkward postures for more than a total of 2-4 hours
  - use of vibrating or impact tools/equipment for more than a total of 2-4 hours during a workshift
  - using forceful hand exertions for more than a total of 2-4 hours at a time

- unassisted frequent or heavy lifting for more than a total of 1-2 hours
- picked signal risk factors based on scientific literature review
- presence of signal risk factor increase probability of potential problems
- additional trigger of one or more work-related musculoskeletal disorder recorded after effective date of the rule

☐ Grandparenting provision: employers with existing, effective programs are exempted from certain provisions. This allows them to continue working to improve jobs rather than shifting gears to repeat activities they have already done

Identification of Problem Jobs

☐ Information on musculoskeletal disorders and reporting procedures should be given to workers exposed to signal risk factors or recorded work-related musculoskeletal disorders.

☐ Risk factor checklist completed for jobs w/signal risk factors or recorded WMSDs:

- checklist is more detailed evaluation of risk factor exposures
- separates jobs that need to be controlled (i.e., problem jobs or those with a checklist score of more than 5)
- OSHA has provided a checklist employers can use - Rule allows alternative evaluations to be used as well

Control of Risk Factor Exposures

☐ Problem jobs have to be controlled (i.e., the checklist score must be reduced to 5 or below).

☐   There are two approaches:

     -    The quick fix (where causes of problem and appropriate controls can be readily identified and implemented)

     -    A job improvement process (where causes are more complicated and additional analysis is needed before controls can be identified and implemented

☐   Engineering or administrative controls supplemented by personal protective equipment (PPE)

☐   Back belts and wrist splints are not considered to be PPE under the rule

☐   Where employees routinely handle heavy packages (>25 lbs) manually, they must be able to determine the relative weight of the package in order to lift or handle appropriately. Can mark the weight or identify contents in a way that would indicate the approximate weight

Ergonomic Design and Controls for New or Changed Jobs

☐   Protect employees in the future; prevent the introduction of problem jobs started or changed after the rule is fully effective.

☐   Most efficient approach is to design out problems up front.

Training

☐   Workers in problem jobs and their supervisors must be trained.

☐   Employers must evaluate the effectiveness of the training program.

Medical Management

☐ Focus on responding to problems and getting employees back to work.

☐ Implement case management rather than medical surveillance.

Phase-In Period for Compliance

☐ Provisions are tiered with different dates for compliance.

☐ Small employers get an additional year to comply with all of the substantive provisions.

References

Aeking, C.A., and R. Kuller. The perception of an interior as a function of its colour, *Ergonomics*, 1972. vol. 15, no. 6, pp. 645-654.

Altman, J.W. Improvements needed in a central store of human performance data, *Human Factors*, 1964, vol. 6. no. 6. pp. 681-686,

Altman, J.W. Classification of human error. in W.B. Askren (ed.), Symposium on reliability of human performance in work, *AMRL*, TR 67-88, May 1967.

Askren, W.B. (ed.). Symposium on reliability of human performance in work, *AMRL*, TR 67-88, May 1967.

Azer, N.Z., P.E. McNall, and H.C. Leung. Effects of heat stress on performance, *Ergonomics*, 1972, vol. 15, no. 6. pp. 68 1-69 1.

Balke, B. Human tolerances, Civil Aeromedical Research Institute, Federal Aviation Agency, Aeronautical Center, Oklahoma City, Report 62-6, April, 1962.

Barany, J.W. The nature of individual differences in bodily forces exerted during a simple motor task, *Journal of Industrial Engineering*, 1963, vol. 14, no. 6, pp. 332-341.

Barnes, R.M., and M.E. Mundell. A study, of simultaneous symmetrical hand motions. University of Iowa, Iowa City, *Studies In Engineering*, Bulletin 17, 1939.

References

Barter, J.T., L. Emanuel, and B. Truett. A statistical evaluation of joint range area data, USAF, WADC, Technical Note 57-311, 1957.

Boggs, D.H., and J.R. Simon. Differential effect of noise on tasks of varying complexity, *Journal of Applied Psychology*, 1968, vol. 52, no. 2, pp. 148-153.

Broadbent, D.E. Effect of noise on an "intellectual" task. *Journal of the Acoustical Society of America*, 1958, vol. 30, pp. 824-827.

Briggs, S.J. A study in the design of work areas, unpublished doctoral dissertation, Purdue University, Lafayette, Indiana, August 1955.

Brouha, L. *Physiology in Industry*, Pergamon Press, New York, 1960.

Brown, J.S., and A.T. Slater-Hammel. Discrete movements in the horizontal plane as a function of their length and direction, *Journal of Experimental Psychology*, 19491. vol, 39. pp. 84-95.

Brown, J.S., E.W. Wieben, and E.B. Norris. Discrete movements toward and away from the body in a horizontal plane, ONR, USN, SDC, Contract N5ori-57, Report 6, September, 1948.

Burger, G.C.E. Heart rate and the concept of circulatory load, *Ergonomics*, 1969, vol. 12. no. 6, pp. 857-864.

Christensen, E.H. Physiological valuation of work in the Nykroppa iron works, in W. F. Floyd and A. T. Welford (eds.), *Ergonomics Society Symposium on Fatigue*, Lewis, London, 1953, pp. 93-108.

Corlett. E. N., and K. Mahadeva: A relationship between a freely chosen working pace and energy consumption curves, *Ergonomics*, 1970, vol. 13, no. 4. pp. 5 17-524.

Corrigan, R.E., and W.J. Brogden: The trigonometric relationship of precision and angle of linear pursuit-movements, *American Journal of Psychology*, 1949, vol. 62, pp. 90-98.

Craik, K.J.W. Psychological and physiological aspects of control mechanisms with special reference to tank gunnery, Part 1. Medical Research Council (Great Britain), Military Personnel Research Committee, B.P.C. 43/254, August 1943.

Damon, A., H.W. Stoudt, and R.A. McFarland: *The Human Body in Equipment Design*, Harvard University Press, Cambridge, Massachusetts, 1966.

Datta, S.R. and N.L. Ramanathan. Ergonomics comparison of seven modes of carrying loads on the horizontal plane, *Ergonomics*, 1971, vol. 14. no. 2. pp. 269-278.

Davies, B.T. Moving loads manually, *Applied Ergonomics*, 1972, vol. 3, no. 4, pp. 190-194.

Davies, C.T.M. Cardiac frequency in relation to aerobic capacity for work, *Ergonomics*, 1968, vol. I, pp. 511-526.

Dempster, W.T. The anthropometry of body action. *Annals of the New York Academy of Sciences*, 1955, vol. 63, pp. 559-585.

Dvorak, A., N.L. Merrick, W.L. Dealey, and G.C. Ford. *Typewriting Behavior*, American Book Company, New, York, 1936.

Edholm, O.G. *The Biology of Work*, World University Library, McGraw-Hill Book Company, New York, 1967.

Ellson. D.G.. and L. Wheeler. The range effect, USAF, Air Materiel Command, Wright-Patterson Air Force Base, TR 4, April 22, 1947.

Faulkner. T.W.. and T.J. Murphy: Illumination: A human factors viewpoint. Paper presented at 15th annual meeting of Human Factors Society, 1971.

Faulkner, T.W., and T.J. Murphy. Lighting for difficult visual tasks, *Human Factors*, 1973, vol. 15. no 2, pp. 149-162.

Gilbreth, F. *Motion Study*, Van Nostrand Company, Inc., New York, 1911.

Glencross, D.J. Temporal organization in a repetitive speed skill, *Ergonomics*, 1973, vol. 16, no. 6. pp. 765-776.

Gordon, E.E. The use of energy costs in regulating physical activity in chronic disease, A.M.A., *Archives of Industrial Health*, November 1957, vol. 16, pp. 437-441.

Gottsdanker, R.M.: The continuation of tapping sequences, *Journal of Psychology*, 1954, vol. 37, pp. 123-132.

Greene, J.H., W.H.M. Morris, and J.E. Wiebers. A method for measuring physiological cost of work, *Journal of Industrial Engineering*, vol. 10. no. 3. May-June]959.

Harris, S.J., and K.U. Smith. Dimensional analysis of motion: VII. Extent and direction of manipulative movements as factors in defining motions, *Journal of Applied Psychology*, 1954. vol. 38. pp. 126-130.

Harston, L.D. Contrasting approaches to the analysis of skilled movements, *Journal of General Psychology*, 1939, vol. 20. pp. 263-293.

Hilgendorf, L.: Information input and response time. *Ergonomics*, 1966, vol. 9, no.1. pp. 31-37.

Hunsicker, P.A. Arm Strength as selected degrees of elbow flexion, USAF, WADC, TR 54-548, August 1955.

International Occupational Safety and Health Information Centre, *Manual Lifting and Carrying*, Geneva, CIS Information Sheet 3, 1962.

Irwin. L.A., J.J. Levitz. and A.M. Freed. Human reliability in the performance of maintenance, in *Proceedings, Symposium on quantification of human performance, Aug, 17-19, 1964*, Albuquerque, New Mexico, pp. 143-198, M-5.7 Subcommittee on Human Factors, Electronic Industries Association.

Johansson. G., and K. Rumar. Drivers' brake reaction times, *Human Factors*, 1971. vol. 13, no. 1, pp. 23-27.

Kalsbeek. J.W.H. Sinus arrhythmia and the dual task of measuring mental load, in W.T. Singleton, J.G. Fox, and D. Whitfield (eds.), *Measurement of Man at Work*, Taylor and Francis, London, 1971, pp. 101-113.

Kalsbeek, J.W.H. Do you believe in sinus arrhythmia? *Ergonomics*, 1973, vol. 16, no. 1, pp. 99-104.

Karger, D.W., and F.H. Bayha. *Engineered Work Measurement*, 2d ed., The Industrial Press, New York, 1965.

Khalil, T.M. An electromyographic methodology for the evaluation of industrial design, *Human Factors*, 1973. vol. 15. no. 3. pp. 257-264.

Kroemer, K.H.E. Human strength: terminology. measurement, and interpretation of data, *Human Factors*, 1970, vol. 12, no. 3, pp. 297-313.

Lauru, L. The measurement of fatigue, *The Manager*, 1954. vol. 22, pp. 299-303 and 369-375.

LeBlanc, J.A. Use of heart rate as an index of work output, *Journal of Applied Physiology*, 1957. vol. 10. PP. 275-280.

Lehmann, G. Physiological measurements as a basis of work organization in industry, Ergonomics, 1958. vol. 1. pp. 328-344.

Luczak, H., and W. Laurig: An analysis of heart rate variability, *Ergonomics*, 1973. vol. 16, no. 1, pp. 85-97.

Manning, P. (ed.). *Office Design: A Study of Environment*, Pilkington Research Unit, Department of Building Science, University of Liverpool, Liverpool, England, SfB (92): UDC 725.23, 1965.

Manning, P. Windows environment and people, Interbuild Arena, October 1967.

Margaria, R.F. Mangili, F. Cuttica, and P. Cerretelli. The kinetics of the oxygen consumption at the onset of muscular exercise in man, *Ergonomics*, 1965, vol. 8, no. 1, pp. 49-54.

Maynard, H.B. *Industrial Engineering Handbook*, 2d ed., McGraw-Hill Book Company, New York, 1963.

Mead, P.G., and P.B. Sampson. Hand steadiness during unrestricted linear arm movements, *Human Factors*, 1972, vol. 14, no. 1. pp. 45-50.

Miles, D.W. Preferred rates in rhythmic response, *Journal of General Psychology*, 1937, vol. 16, pp. 427-469.

Monod, Par H. La validite des mesures de frequence cardiaque en ergonomie, *Ergonomics*, 1967, vol. 10, no. 5, pp. 485-537.

Murrell, K.F.H. *Human Performance in Industry*, Reinhold Publishing Corporation, New York, 1965.

Passmore, R. Daily energy expenditure by man, *Proceedings of the Nutrition Society*, 1956, vol. 15, pp. 83-89.

Passmore, R., and J.V.G.A. Durnin. Human energy expenditure, *Physiological Reviews*, 1955, vol. 35, pp. 801-875.

Pattie, C. *Simulated Tractor Overturnings: A Study of Human Responses in an Emergency Situation*, Ph.D. thesis, Purdue University, May 1973.

Provins, K.A. Effect of limb position on the forces exerted about the elbow and shoulder joints on the two sides simultaneously, *Journal of Applied Physiology*, 1955, vol. 7, pp. 387-389.

Provins, K.A., and N. Salter. Maximum torque exerted about the elbow joint, *Journal of Applied Physiology*, 1955, vol, 7, pp. 393-398.

Salter, N., and H.D. Darcus: The effect of the degree of elbow flexion on maximum torques developed in pronation and supination of the right hand, *Journal of Anatomy*, 1952, vol. 86, pp. 197-202.

Salvendy, G., and J. Pilitsis. Psychophysiological aspects of paced and unpaced performance as influenced by age, *Ergonomics*, 1971, vol. 14, no. 6, pp. 703-71 1.

Schappe, R.H. Motion element synthesis: an assessment, *Perceptual and Motor Skills*, 1965, vol. 20, pp. 103-106.

Schmidtke, H., and F. Stier. Der aufbau komplexer bewegungsablaufe aus elementarbewegungen, *Forschungsberichte des landes Nordrhein-Westfalen*, 1960. no. 822. pp. 13-32.

Shephard, R.J. Comments on "Cardiac frequency in relation to aerobic capacity for work", *Ergonomics*, 1970, vol, 13. no. 4, pp. 509-513.

Singleton, W.T. The measurement of man at work with particular reference to arousal, in W. J. Singleton, J. G. Fox, and D. Whitfield (eds.), *Measurements of Man at Work*, Taylor and Francis, London, 1971. pp. 17-25.

Snook, S.H. The effects of age and physique on continuous-work capacity, *Human Factors*, 1971, vol. 13, no. 5, pp. 467-479.

Snook, S.H., and C.H. Irvine, Psychophysical studies of physiological fatigue criteria, *Human Factors*, 1969, vol.I, no. 3. pp. 291-300.

Snook, S.H., C.H. Irvine, and S.F. Bass. *Maximum weights and workloads acceptable to male industrial workers while performing lifting, lowering, pulling, carrying, and walking tasks*, paper presented to American Industrial Hygiene Conference, Denver, May. 1969.

Switzer, S.A. Weight lifting capabilities of a selected sample of human males, AMRL, MRL, TDR 62-57, 1962.

Tichauer, E.R. A pilot study of the biomechanics of lifting in simulated industrial work situations, *Journal of Safety Research*, September, 1971, vol. 3, no. 3. pp. 98-115.

Tuttle, W.W., and B.A. Schottelius. *Textbook of Physiology*, 16th ed., The C. V. Mosby Company, St. Louis, 1969.

Vince, M.A. The intermittency of control movements and the psychological refractory period, *British Journal of Psychology*, 1948, vol. 38, pp. 149-157.

Vos, H.W. Physical workload in different body postures, while working near to, or below ground level, *Ergonomics*, 1973, vol. 16. no. 6, pp. 817-828.

Wargo, M.J.: Human operator response speed, frequency, and flexibility: a review and analysis, *Human Factors*, 1967, vol. 9, no. 3. pp. 221-238.

Warrick, M.J., A.W. Kibler, and D.A. Topmiller. Response time to unexpected stimuli, *Human Factors*, 1965, vol. 7, no. 1, pp. 81-86.

Wehrkamp, R., and K. U. Smith: Dimensional analysis of motion: II. Travel-distance effects, *Journal of Applied Psychology*, 1952, vol. 36. pp. 201-206.

Young, L. C. A study of tremor in normal subjects, *Journal of Experimental Psychology*, 1933, vol. 16. pp. 644-656.

Glossary

Abduction: Movement away from the body midline. For example, shoulder abduction refers to the movement of the elbow away from the body, resulting in an increased angle at the shoulder joint. Adduction is the opposite term.

Accessibility: The ease with which parts can be accessed when performing a preventive maintenance or repair activity.

ANSI: The American National Standards Institute. ANSI has been responsible for the development of design guidelines for computer workstations (ANSI/HFS 100-1988), and draft guidelines for ergonomics (ANSI Z365).

Analog Display: A display requiring some level of interpretation of information on the part of the user. For example, a temperature gauge that has colored zones indicating acceptable and unacceptable temperature regions is an analog display. The opposite of an analog display is a digital display.

Anti-Fatigue Mats: Mats or padding on the floor designed to reduce stresses on the feet and leg across the work shift. Cushioned insoles for shoes can be viewed as "portable anti-fatigue mats".

Anthropometry: The study and measurement of human physical dimensions.

Awkward Posture: Any fixed or constrained body position that overloads muscles and tendons or loads joints in an uneven or assymmetrical manner.

Biomechanics: The study of the effects of internal and external forces on the human body in movement and at rest.

Biomechanical: Biomechanical models calculate physical stresses occurring at the discs in the low back and a various body joints. The stresses are compared with accepted limits for compressive forces.

Bursitis: Bursae are lubricating pads separating tendons from bones in parts of the body. Bursitis is the result of the inflammation of a bursae. The inflammation may be caused by repetitive or forceful exertions at that joint.

Carpal Tunnel Syndrome: A specific CTD occurring as the result of compression on the median nerve that travels through the carpal tunnel in the wrist. Symptoms can include tingling and numbness in the hand, and loss of dexterity and strength in the hand.

Contact Stress: Exposure of a body part to a hard or sharp surface/edge at a workstation or tool. Contact stress has been associated with the development of CTDs.

Contrast: Difference between the lighter and darker areas of (e.g.) a computer monitor.

Control: Any device manipulated by the user that allows the user to interact with the system.

Coupling: The interface between the hands and an object lifted or control manipulated.

CTD: A cumulative trauma disorder (CTD) is a bodily injury caused by the build up of mechanical stressors that build up over time. Specifically, it is a health disorder arising from repeated biomechanical stress due to ergonomic hazards.

DWM: Damaging Wrist Motions (DWMS) are defined as hand motions coupled with force.

Deviation: Movement of a body part towards the extreme in its range of motion. For example, ulnar deviation of the wrist described the movement of the wrist away from a straight position towards the ulna bone in the forearm.

Disability: Under the Americans with Disabilities Act (ADA), an individual with a disability is a person who has a physical or mental impairment that substantially limits one or more major life activity; has a record of such an impairment; or is regarded as having such an impairment.

Display: A device that provides feedback to an operator regarding the status of a machine. Displays can take many different forms and can use different sense modalities (vision, hearing) to provide their feedback.

Duration: The continuous time a task is performed without a sufficient rest period.

Ergonomics: A discipline dealing with the interaction between the worker and the work environment.

Ergonomic Hazards: Workplace conditions that pose a biomechanical stress to the worker.

Ergonomics Program: Application of ergonomics in a structured system including the following components: health and risk factor surveillance, job analysis and design, medical management, and training.

Extension: Movement at a joint that increases the angle at that joint.

Flexion: Movement at a joint that reduces the angle at that joint.

Flicker (Refresh Rate): The perceived movement of characters on the screen. Flicker can be a function of the refresh rate of the display, defined as the number of times per second that an electron beam returns to a defined point on the screen to re-excite the phosphor and repaint the screen.

Fonts: Types of character designs used in labels, computer monitors, etc.

Footrest: A high load task or constrained body position that overloads muscles and tendons or loads joints in an uneven or assymetrical manner.

Forearm Rotation: Rotational movement of the forearm at the elbow joint (e.g., when working a screwdriver). Rotating the forearm such that the palm of the hand is facing down is referred to as pronation. Rotating the forearm such that the palm is up is referred to as supination.

Functional Working Height: The actual position of the hands when performing a task. Depending on the height of the objects handled, the functional working height may not be the same as the shelf or workstation height.

Health Surveillance: Component of an ergonomics program consisting of the ongoing and systematic collection and analysis of health and exposure data. Consists of both active and passive surveillance and is used to quantify the presence and magnitude of injury and ergonomic issues in jobs.

Heat Stress: Exposure to a hot environment that reduces the capability for sustained activity and speeds up fatigue.

Horizontal Line of Sight: A horizontal line drawn from the eye of the worker. Workers should not have to perform intensive visual activities above the horizontal line of sight.

Illuminance: A measure of the amount of light falling on or incident to a defined surface (typically measured in lux or footcandles). Luminance is a corresponding measure of the amount of light emitted from a light source.

Incidence Rate: The number of injuries (incidents) that occur over a period of time, typically expressed as the number of incidents per 200,000 worker hours.

L5/SI: The intervertebral disc between the 5th lumbar (L5) and Ist sacral (SI) vertebrae of the spinal column.

Ligaments: Fibrous structures that connect bones to bones within the body, providing support while allowing flexibility and movement.

Lux: A measure of illuminance. One lux equals 0.093 footcandles.

Maintainability: Equipment design focused on the achievement of some specific capability.

Maintenance: All of the technical activities that are devoted to the upkeep of equipment.

Major Life Activity: Activities that an average person can perform with little or no difficulty. Examples are: walking, speaking, breathing, performing manual tasks, seeing, hearing, learning, caring for oneself, working, sitting, standing, lifting, and reading. These are examples only.

MMH: Manual Materials Handling (MMH) refers to any handling task involving the human body as the "power source". MMH includes lifting, lowering, pushing, pulling, carrying, and holding.

Median Nerve: The nerve that travels through the carpal tunnel of the wrist and services the thumb and first three fingers of the hand. Compression of the median nerve is the definition of carpal tunnel syndrome.

Mental Impairment: A mental impairment is defined by the ADA as "[a]ny mental or psychological disorder, such as mental retardation, organic brain syndrome, emotional or mental illness, and specific learning disabilities."

Muscle Sprain: A torn muscle fiber. Typically the tear is microscopic.

Neutral Posture: The body position that minimizes stresses on the body. Typically the neutral posture will be near the mid-range of any joint's range of motion.

NIOSH Equation: The National Institute of Occupational Safety and Health (NIOSH) 1981 and 1991 guidelines consist of a series of mathematical equations developed based on historical injury data and related job data. The equations calculate recommended maximum safe weights of lift.

Optimal Viewing Angle: The range from the horizontal viewing distance down to 45 degrees below horizontal.

Physical Impairment: A physical impairment is defined by the ADA as "[a]ny disorder, or condition, cosmetic disfigurement, or anatomical loss affecting one or more of the following body systems: neurological, musculoskeletal, special sense organs, respiratory (including speech organs), cardiovascular, reproductive, digestive, genito-urinary, hemic and lymphatic, skin, and endocrine."

Pinch Grip: One of several types of grips that do not allow the hand to fully encircle the object being handled. Pinch grip types include tip pinches (tip of thumb against tip of index finger), pulp pinches (flat surface of thumb against flat surface of index finger), lateral pinches (thumb against side of index finger as when turning a key), and others.

Pixel: One of several dots that compose a character on a VDT.

Polarity: Standard polarity on a screen is light characters on a dark background. Reverse polarity is dark characters on a light background.

Power Grip: A grip allowing the four fingers and thumb to encircle the object. This grip will generally maximize power on the part of the worker.

Pronation: Rotation of the forearm such that the palm faces down or back.

Psychophysical: Psychophysical data are collected by having subjects select their maximum acceptable weight of handling under experimental conditions. Subjects adjust the weight handled until they feel the weight is not excessive. These selected weights represent design guidelines.

Range of Motion: The limits of movement defined at a joint or landmark of the body. Stresses on the connective tissues at a joint increase as the joint moves towards the limit of its range of motion.

RPE: Rate of Perceived Exertion is a scale filled out by workers which allows them to estimate the level of physical exertion associated with a task.

Repetition Rate: The average number of movements or exertions performed by a joint or a body link within a unit of time.

RWL: Recommended Weight of Lift (RWL) is computed using the NIOSH equation. The RWL reflects the weight that can be safely handled by 99% of males and 75% of females based on the task conditions.

Resonance: The tendency of the human body to act in concert with externally generated vibration at selected vibration frequencies and actually amplify the incoming vibration and exacerbate its effects.

Rest Period: A contiguous period of time not spent performing any tasks. This may be a lunch break or a work break. Part of the measure of recovery time.

Risk Factors: Conditions of a job, process, or operation that contribute to the risk of developing CTDs ... Risk factors are regarded as synergistic elements of ergonomic hazards which must be considered in light of their combined effect in inducing CTDS.

rms (root-mean-square): The square root of the average value of the square of the acceleration record; rms is the preferred method of quantifying the severity of human vibration exposures based on the convenience of measurements and analysis and the harmonization with some other areas of engineering.

Sharp Edge: An edge on a work surface that applies pressure to the wrist, forearm, or elbow of the worker when it is resting on it. An operational criteria (in terms of radius of curvature) for what constitutes a sharp edge is not available in the literature.

Sit/Stand: A workstation that enables the worker to perform tasks at a standing position while still providing some support of a seated workstation.

Static Load: Stresses on the body increase as a function of body parts remaining immobile for extended periods.

Supination: Rotation of the forearm such that the palm faces up or out.

Tendinitis: Tendons connect muscles to bones. Tendinitis is the result of the inflammation of tendons at a body part.

Tenosynovitis: Swelling and inflammation of the sheath that surrounds certain tendons. The sheath produces a lubricating fluid for the tendon; tenosynovitis results from a decreased capacity to produce this lubricating fluid.

Tool Balancers: Any type of external support for a tool (or object) that eliminates or reduces the amount of weight supported by the worker.

Trigger Finger: Tendons in the finger joints can swell due to overuse, "locking" the finger into a fixed position.

Troubleshooting: The decision making process used by maintenance personnel to locate the source of a maintenance problem.

Vibration: Whole body vibration is vibration transmitted to the entire body through some support such as a vehicular seat or building floor. Segmental vibration is vibration locally applied to specific body parts such as the hands and arms from a vibrating hand tool.

Vibration White Finger: A condition where the blood vessels in the hand constrict, resulting in decreased blood flow. This disease is associated with the long-term use of vibrating tools (or in general exposure to vibration). Also referred to as Raynaud's phenomenon.

Vertebral Disc: Discs separate the bones that make up the spinal column. They are fibrous structures filled with a pulpy, gelatinous matter. They function as shock absorbers for the spine. Disc-related injuries to the back result from deformation of the discs, including bulging and rupturing of the discs.

VDT: Video Display Terminal (computer monitor).

Warning: Specific stimuli which alert a user to the presence of a hazard, thereby triggering processing Of additional information regarding the nature, probability, and magnitude of the hazard. This additional information may be within the user's memory or may be provided by other sources external to the user.

Work Cycle: The work cycle consists of an exertion period and a recovery (or smaller' exertion) period necessary to complete one sequence of a task, before the sequence is repeated. The work cycle may consist of several elements, such as move, place, and fasten.

Work Cycle Recovery Period: The time not spent performing a movement(s) or exertion(s) within one work cycle.

Workstation: The entire area accessed by a worker when performing a specific task or job cycle.

Index

Government Institutes Mini-Catalog

PC #	ENVIRONMENTAL TITLES	Pub Date	Price
629	ABCs of Environmental Regulation: Understanding the Fed Regs	1998	$49
627	ABCs of Environmental Science	1998	$39
585	Book of Lists for Regulated Hazardous Substances, 8th Edition	1997	$79
579	Brownfields Redevelopment	1998	$79
4088	CFR Chemical Lists on CD ROM, 1997 Edition	1997	$125
4089	Chemical Data for Workplace Sampling & Analysis, Single User Disk	1997	$125
512	Clean Water Handbook, 2nd Edition	1996	$89
581	EH&S Auditing Made Easy	1997	$79
587	E H & S CFR Training Requirements, 3rd Edition	1997	$89
4082	EMMI-Envl Monitoring Methods Index for Windows-Network	1997	$537
4082	EMMI-Envl Monitoring Methods Index for Windows-Single User	1997	$179
525	Environmental Audits, 7th Edition	1996	$79
548	Environmental Engineering and Science: An Introduction	1997	$79
643	Environmental Guide to the Internet, 4th Edition	1998	$59
560	Environmental Law Handbook, 14th Edition	1997	$79
353	Environmental Regulatory Glossary, 6th Edition	1993	$79
625	Environmental Statutes, 1998 Edition	1998	$69
4098	Environmental Statutes Book/CD-ROM, 1998 Edition	1997	$208
4994	Environmental Statutes on Disk for Windows-Network	1997	$405
4994	Environmental Statutes on Disk for Windows-Single User	1997	$139
570	Environmentalism at the Crossroads	1995	$39
536	ESAs Made Easy	1996	$59
515	Industrial Environmental Management: A Practical Approach	1996	$79
510	ISO 14000: Understanding Environmental Standards	1996	$69
551	ISO 14001: An Executive Report	1996	$55
588	International Environmental Auditing	1998	$149
518	Lead Regulation Handbook	1996	$79
478	Principles of EH&S Management	1995	$69
554	Property Rights: Understanding Government Takings	1997	$79
582	Recycling & Waste Mgmt Guide to the Internet	1997	$49
603	Superfund Manual, 6th Edition	1997	$115
566	TSCA Handbook, 3rd Edition	1997	$95
534	Wetland Mitigation: Mitigation Banking and Other Strategies	1997	$75

PC #	SAFETY and HEALTH TITLES	Pub Date	Price
547	Construction Safety Handbook	1996	$79
553	Cumulative Trauma Disorders	1997	$59
559	Forklift Safety	1997	$65
539	Fundamentals of Occupational Safety & Health	1996	$49
612	HAZWOPER Incident Command	1998	$59
535	Making Sense of OSHA Compliance	1997	$59
589	Managing Fatigue in Transportation, *ATA Conference*	1997	$75
558	PPE Made Easy	1998	$79
598	Project Mgmt for E H & S Professionals	1997	$59
552	Safety & Health in Agriculture, Forestry and Fisheries	1997	$125
613	Safety & Health on the Internet, 2nd Edition	1998	$49
597	Safety Is A People Business	1997	$49
463	Safety Made Easy	1995	$49
590	Your Company Safety and Health Manual	1997	$79

Government Institutes
4 Research Place, Suite 200 • Rockville, MD 20850-3226
Tel. (301) 921-2323 • FAX (301) 921-0264
Email: giinfo@govinst.com • Internet: http://www.govinst.com

Please call our customer service department at (301) 921-2323 for a free publications catalog.

CFRs now available online. Call (301) 921-2355 for info.

GOVERNMENT INSTITUTES ORDER FORM

4 Research Place, Suite 200 • Rockville, MD 20850-3226
Tel (301) 921-2323 • Fax (301) 921-0264
Internet: http://www.govinst.com • E-mail: giinfo@govinst.com

3 EASY WAYS TO ORDER

1. Phone: **(301) 921-2323**
Have your credit card ready when you call.

2. Fax: **(301) 921-0264**
Fax this completed order form with your company
purchase order or credit card information.

3. Mail: **Government Institutes**
4 Research Place, Suite 200
Rockville, MD 20850-3226   USA
Mail this completed order form with a check, company
purchase order, or credit card information.

PAYMENT OPTIONS

❑ **Check** (payable to Government Institutes in US dollars)

❑ **Purchase Order** (This order form must be attached to your company
P.O. Note: All International orders must be prepaid.)

❑ **Credit Card**   ❑ VISA   ❑ MasterCard   ❑ AMERICAN EXPRESS

Exp.___/____

Credit Card No. _____

Signature _____

(Government Institutes' Federal I.D.# is 52-0994196)

CUSTOMER   INFORMATION

Ship To: (Please attach your purchase order)

Name: _____

GI Account # (7 digits on mailing label): _____

Company/Institution: _____

Address: _____
(Please supply street address for UPS shipping)

_____

City: _____ State/Province: _____

Zip/Postal Code: _____ Country: _____

Tel: (____) _____

Fax: (____) _____

Email Address: _____

Bill To: (if different from ship-to address)

Name: _____

Title/Position: _____

Company/Institution: _____

Address: _____
(Please supply street address for UPS shipping)

_____

City: _____ State/Province: _____

Zip/Postal Code: _____ Country: _____

Tel: (____) _____

Fax: (____) _____

Email Address: _____

Qty.	Product Code	Title	Price

❑ **New Edition No Obligation Standing Order Program**

Please enroll me in this program for the products I have ordered. Government
Institutes will notify me of new editions by sending me an invoice. I understand
that there is no obligation to purchase the product. This invoice is simply my
reminder that a new edition has been released.

15 DAY MONEY-BACK GUARANTEE

If you're not completely satisfied with any product, return it undamaged within
15 days for a full and immediate refund on the price of the product.

Subtotal _____

MD Residents add 5% Sales Tax _____

Shipping and Handling (see box below) _____

Total Payment Enclosed _____

Within U.S:	**Outside U.S:**
1-4 products: $6/product	Add $15 for each item (Airmail)
5 or more: $3/product	Add $10 for each item (Surface)

SOURCE CODE: BP01